AS History
UNIT 2

OCR

Module 2584: Britain, 1899–1964

Andrew Holland

Series Editor: Derrick Murphy

Philip Allan Updates
Market Place
Deddington
Oxfordshire
OX15 0SE

tel: 01869 338652
fax: 01869 337590
e-mail: sales@philipallan.co.uk
www.philipallan.co.uk

ISBN 0 86003 734 7

This Guide has been written specifically to support students preparing for the OCR AS History Unit 2 examination. The content has been neither approved nor endorsed by OCR and remains the sole responsibility of the author.

Printed by Information Press, Eynsham, Oxford

Contents

Introduction

Aims

This unit guide covers British history in the period 1899–1964. After studying Module 2584 students should have a good knowledge and understanding of a range of historical developments that happened during this time. The specification for this option is divided into four study topics, namely:

(1) Liberals and Labour, 1899–1918
(2) Interwar domestic problems, 1918–39
(3) Foreign policy, 1939–63
(4) Postwar Britain, 1945–64

The Content Guidance section deals with the key issues for each study topic. You will be assessed by way of a 45-minute-long essay-based examination. Two questions are set, each relating to one of the key issues. You are asked to choose one. The unit is worth 30% of your final marks if you are studying to AS only and 15% if you intend to go for the full A-level.

The study of A-level history requires that you build on skills acquired at GCSE and learn new ones. At A-level there tends to be more emphasis on the production of essays or extended writing. Crucial to this is the ability to write in a clear, logical, concise, well-structured and relevant manner. In particular, you should ensure that you stick to the question and do not drift into a narrative about the topic you are presented with. This is absolutely necessary to gain the highest grades. AS history questions also demand specific skills related to evaluation, i.e. weighing up a range of historical material and arriving at a balanced conclusion. And, of course, all of this has to be done eventually under tight time constraints.

Throughout your first year of study your teachers are likely to encourage you to improve your note-taking skills and to read widely. Reading a range of materials will greatly improve your ability to write effectively. As a general guide, when preparing for essays, start by reading short, simple basic texts and move towards the more complicated. You should attempt to use three or four different sources for each piece of work, which may include journal and/or internet articles, basic textbooks and more specialist texts. This will widen your knowledge and make exam-type essays easy to tackle.

Planning, researching and writing takes considerable time and you must be prepared to stick to a study timetable. As a rough guide, you should spend the same amount of time each week on studying AS history at home as you receive in the form of classroom tuition. Your teacher should help you with managing time by providing you with:
- a copy of the study topic details and assessment information
- a scheme of work that tells you how and when the content of the study topic will be covered

Use these documents carefully and methodically and you will reap dividends.

How to use this guide

This guide is designed to help you with revision and make you fully prepared to achieve the highest of grades in the final examination. It should be used in conjunction with a range of other resources. There are three sections, as follows:

- **Introduction** — this section outlines the assessment objectives of the option, i.e. what knowledge and understanding examiners expect you to display to be successful in the examination. There are also tips on revision and preparation for the final assessment.
- **Content Guidance** — this section gives a review of the four study topics in the option. It deals with some of the more tricky concepts and ideas you will need to get to grips with.
- **Questions and Answers** — this section provides sample essays of band-I and band-III standards on each of the four study topics. There are examiner comments, which indicate the strengths and weaknesses of answers and how extra marks could have been gained.

Revision planning

How you plan your revision time will depend partly on when you will sit the examination for this module (January or June) and how it fits in with the examinations of modules for other subjects. As there are many separate module examinations it is vital that you have a detailed but flexible revision plan drafted well in advance. Before doing this, however, it is important to understand the meaning of revision as opposed to review and recall.

Revision

This should start from the time of your very first lesson and involves reading through notes, handouts and chapters in books to clarify knowledge and understanding. You *must* ensure that you are clear about basic ideas and concepts as you progress from class to class. Revising your study materials and asking teachers for clarification leads to fewer gaps in your basic understanding and helps you memorise factual information more easily.

Reviewing

This involves going over study topic materials once you have been taught the topic content. You may find it useful to use the following approach:

Step 1

Set aside a period within your overall review plan to deal with one key issue at a time, i.e. morning, afternoon or evening review session.

Step 2

Read through your course notes once or twice to remind yourself of the nature of the key issue. You may need to reread handouts, photocopied articles and chapters in texts. If you have revised (see above), this should prove to be a relatively easy task.

Step 3

Make notes of your notes. This does not mean copying out notes in full. You should be able to summarise course notes into key points using minimal text. Do this by using abbreviations, numbering and lettering, bullet points, headings, and different colours for different parts of the key issue.

Review notes can be made in different formats, for example:
- on a sheet of A4 paper, although you should, if using this method, discipline yourself to use only one side per key issue
- on index cards, using one card for each part of the content of each key issue
- in 'mind map', spider web or diagrammatic form on a sheet of paper

You may find it beneficial to use mnemonics. These are words that are formed from the first letters of other key words, terms and phrases. They can help you to summarise vast amounts of information (but you have to be able to remember what the mnemonic stands for!) and improve your memory (see below).

Overall, it is important that review notes are kept brief and should be the main source of information in the process of recall.

Recall

This is the process that involves testing your memory. There are many techniques that can be used to improve memory, such as mnemonics, visualisation (associating words and terms with visual images) and even linking historical material with music. To test your memory the following methods can be used.

Brainstorming

When you have completed the review process, try writing down the main parts of a key issue without looking at your review notes. This can be done even more effectively by linking the material to a past examination question.

Testing each other

Discuss topics with a fellow history student and test each other. Try devising your own exam-type questions.

Essay plans

Without using notes, practise writing plans for essays set on past exam papers. Use a spider web/diagrammatic approach rather than a linear (straight list) format.

Introductions and conclusions

It is useful to practise writing beginnings and endings to past examination questions, as this helps you focus on the requirements of the questions and how to set out your line of argument.

Short essays

Try writing essays using past exam questions in 20 minutes rather than 45 minutes. This makes you write concisely and relevantly, both of which are key requirements for high-grade answers.

Examinable skills

You need to be clear about what you will be tested on in the final examination. In this module there are three assessment objectives (AOs).

- AO1a expects you to recall, select and deploy historical knowledge accurately and to communicate knowledge and understanding of history in a clear and effective manner.
- AO1b asks you to present historical explanations showing understanding of appropriate concepts and arriving at substantial judgements.
- AO2 involves looking at historical context, requiring you to interpret, evaluate and use a range of source material and to explain and evaluate interpretations of the historical events and topics studied.

Essay writing

Writing good essays involves using continuous prose and accurate grammar, punctuation and spelling. Develop a style that is clear, concise and logical. The following tips may help.

- Always begin by analysing the question. Identify:
  (1) the examiner's instruction (e.g. 'Explain...', 'To what extent...')
  (2) the topic (e.g. Liberal social reforms, 1906–14)
  (3) key words and terms that may need defining (e.g. modern welfare state)
- You must plan your answer. Take a maximum of 5 minutes over this. Use a spider web or 'mind map' plan so that you can spread your ideas out, rather than a linear plan.
- Stick closely to the question asked and provide a balanced response, particularly to questions that invite you to discuss different viewpoints (e.g. 'To what extent...', 'How far do you agree with...'). You do not simply have to agree with the assumption behind a question. Consider the following question:

To what extent were the Liberal social reforms of 1906–14 a result of pressure from the Labour movement?

The core of your answer might look at how or why the reforms were a result of pressure from the Labour movement, but you would be wise to look at other influencing factors, such as 'new liberalism', the late nineteenth-century social surveys and economic rivalry. Your conclusion would weigh up all of the issues and identify what appears to be the most significant.

- Avoid signposting (stating the obvious) and writing in the first person (e.g. 'I think...'). Use other lead-in phrases, such as 'It would appear that...' or 'It is argued that...'.
- As a general guide, aim to fill about four sides of paper in your examination booklet (excluding your plan). If you write less, your answer is likely to be thin, lacking detailed supporting material. If you write more, your answer will probably consist mainly of narrative and description that drifts away from the focus of the question.

Essay structure

Essays must have structure so that a line of argument can easily be followed. They can be divided into three parts:

(1) Introduction

(2) Main body

(3) Conclusion

Introduction

Use about two sentences to 'set the scene' or provide the context for your answer. Two or three more sentences should be used to outline your plan of attack on the question. A final sentence can be deployed to link in with the first paragraph of the main body of the essay.

Main body

This will provide the thrust of your argument. As a rough guide, make a separate point in each paragraph, remembering that one sentence does not constitute a paragraph. You may have noticed that the historians whose work you find easiest to follow are those who make a key point or argument at the beginning of a paragraph and then back it up with 'evidence'. The exact content of each paragraph and how the paragraphs link together will depend on the type of question asked.

Conclusion

Avoid simply repeating what you have said in your introduction or the main body of your essay. Attempt to make an overall judgement based on the arguments you have presented. There will be no 'right' answer to the question; you will be assessed on the quality of your reasoning and the evaluation of material you have used.

Be aware that examiners are told to bear in mind the following factors when marking:

- Most candidates have only studied a module for about 10 weeks, with 4–5 hours tuition per week.
- Most candidates have moved to A-level study straight from GCSE. It is a big step up and after only 1 year of study they are not expected to write in a highly mature and sophisticated manner akin to the work produced by an undergraduate.
- A general mark scheme should be adhered to; this is geared towards the assessment of skills and not copious amounts of detailed fact.
- Forty-five minutes is not long to show what you know about a key issue area from the study topic.

Examiners are on your side. They will be looking to see whether your answers are the best you could possibly provide given the circumstances under which you have been working. Even for the highest of grades they do not expect something resembling a perfect answer.

Content
Guidance

The aim of this section is to give you an outline of the key points you will need to know for each study topic. The four study topics in this option are:

(1) Liberals and Labour, 1899–1918
(2) Interwar domestic problems, 1918–39
(3) Foreign policy, 1939–63
(4) Postwar Britain, 1945–64

In turn, each topic is divided into four key issues.

The examination paper will contain a choice of eight questions, two on each study topic. You will have to answer one of these. Each question will focus on a particular key issue.

Liberals and Labour, 1899–1918

The four key issues for study and examination are:

(1) What was the significance of the Liberal election victory of 1906?

(2) How far was the First World War responsible for the growth of the Labour Party and the decline of the Liberal Party?

(3) To what extent was a modern welfare state created by the Liberals between 1906 and 1914?

(4) How serious was the crisis in Britain over the issue of Ireland from 1909 to 1916?

What was the significance of the Liberal election victory of 1906?

Summary

In 1906 the Liberals won a dramatic election victory after nearly 20 years of Conservative domination of British politics. You need to be aware that there is much debate over the extent of this success and also as to why it happened. Although the Liberals gained an impressive number of seats in Parliament, a substantial proportion of the population still voted Conservative. Nevertheless, the Conservative Party did not do as well as it hoped, due mainly to a leadership that appeared out of touch with the needs of the majority of the nation. The Liberals gained in popularity, especially after the Second Boer War (1899–1902), despite campaigning on issues that were not new or forward-looking, such as free trade. The social reform programme that emerged after they had established themselves in power had barely been mentioned in the months preceding the 1906 election.

Before looking at these issues in more detail, note that at the end of the nineteenth century and in the first two decades of the twentieth, the Conservative Party was often referred to as the Unionist Party. This was due to many members firmly believing in the merits of the union of Ireland with Great Britain (i.e. the United Kingdom). There were other politicians who were still intent on pushing for Home Rule.

The problems facing the Conservatives from 1899 to 1905

The problems faced by the Conservatives during this period relate mainly to the leadership of the party. Lord Salisbury was leader and prime minister from 1885 to 1902 and his nephew, Arthur Balfour, from 1902 to 1905.

Salisbury served during his third (1895–1900) and fourth (1900–02) ministries as the last of the aristocratic leaders. He brought to office a strong belief in the need to preserve and protect the rights of the landed classes. He seemed to have little interest in the plight of ordinary working people, which was reflected in an indifferent approach to domestic affairs. To some extent fortune smiled upon Salisbury, as by the end of the nineteenth century there had been something of an economic revival and there had been considerable success during the first year of the Second Boer War. This partly explains the resounding victory of the Conservatives at the 'khaki' election of 1900.

Although Salisbury was more concerned with foreign affairs, some notable reforms were implemented at home before the 1900 election. These included the **Land Act** (1896), an **Education Act** and the **Workmen's Compensation Act** (both 1897) and the introduction of **county councils** (1888). Generally, though, Salisbury aimed to save rather than spend government money so that taxation and rates could be kept low.

By 1902 Salisbury lacked the drive to continue and his health was failing. He was replaced by his nephew Arthur Balfour, who was more of a reformer but shared his uncle's aristocratic Anglican traditionalism. He was intelligent and astute but had little enthusiasm for tackling a number of burning issues that started to emerge. Although the economy had picked up, there was still concern within the nation as a whole that there would be further slumps to match those of the great depression years of the late nineteenth century. There was also worry over the poor working and living conditions still being experienced by the masses, as revealed in the social surveys of **Booth** and **Rowntree**, and shockingly high infant mortality rates. This all related to the question of 'national efficiency' and whether Britain was in a fit state to rule an empire and maintain its worldwide economic and political status.

Balfour clearly understood the problems relating to national efficiency and made an attempt to deal with them. Three reforms were of note:
- **The Education Act, 1902:** this placed control of primary and secondary education with the county and county borough councils. This included the old voluntary schools (Church of England and Catholic), which would be financed out of state funds. This inevitably caused great opposition from nonconformists.
- **The Licensing Act, 1904:** this gave compensation to publicans who were refused a renewal of their licence. Again, this was opposed by nonconformists, many of whom had campaigned against the evils of liquor.
- **The Unemployed Workmen Act, 1905:** this allowed 'distress committees' to be set up which would help unemployed people find work. There was no provision for emergency relief, however, and the act was seen as being ineffective.

There were some problems that the Conservatives seemed to exacerbate during this period:
- **The Taff Vale case, 1901:** a strike by workers on the Taff Vale Railway in South Wales in 1901 greatly angered the owners who lost money. The company decided to sue the Amalgamated Society of Railway Servants for compensation and was duly awarded £23,000. Union leaders and members were scared that future strikes would prove to be financially disastrous. They took a very dim view of the fact that Balfour fully supported the judgement.

- **Chinese slavery, 1902–04:** there was a shortage of labour in South Africa as a result of the Second Boer War. The British High Commissioner, Milner, pushed the government to sanction the use of Chinese workers, which it did. The labourers were treated appallingly and there was a moral outcry.
- **The Second Boer War, 1899–1902:** although the war had begun well, it turned into a nightmare as the British resorted to the use of thousands of troops, a 'scorched-earth' policy and concentration camps to defeat the Boers. Even then, the Boers' guerrilla tactics made British victory difficult and there was general concern about the condition of British troops and their ability to win such a conflict.
- **Tariff reform, 1903–05:** the Conservative (Unionist) minister, **Joseph Chamberlain**, campaigned for the need to reintroduce tariffs to protect British manufacturers against foreign competition but giving special treatment to countries in the empire. This went against the ideas of those who treasured the free-trade philosophy, which had made Britain great, and caused a split in the Conservatives. In 1903 Chamberlain resigned but Balfour, on balance, seemed to sympathise with his views.

With hindsight, these problems were not handled very well and they caused much consternation among members of the working class, who believed that living and working conditions were being further damaged by an uncaring Conservative government. The Liberals were bound to gain from these errors of judgement.

The growing popularity of the Liberals

At the beginning of the twentieth century the Liberals lacked strong leadership, unity and financial resources. During Balfour's government, however, their fortunes revived. One reason for this was the **1903 pact** between the Liberals and the **Labour Representation Committee** (LRC), whereby each party would not oppose the other in forthcoming elections in areas considered to be Liberal or Labour strongholds.

Secondly, tariff reform caused some members of the middle classes to doubt the wisdom of the Conservatives and they changed allegiance to the Liberals. The Liberals exploited this situation and also made much of the difficulties experienced during the Second Boer War. This rising level of support was reflected in the election result of 1906.

The Liberal victory of 1905–06

Balfour resigned in December 1905 in the belief that the Conservatives would return to power as the Liberals were still in disarray as a result of divided opinion over the legitimacy of the Second Boer War. The result was astonishing:

Liberals	377 seats (184 in 1900)
Conservatives (Unionists)	157 seats (402 in 1900)

This was regarded as a landslide victory, with the Conservatives left with their smallest number of seats since 1832. The numbers voting Conservative had actually remained roughly the same compared with 1900, but for the Liberals there had been a dramatic increase, probably from voters who had abstained in previous elections.

There appear to be three main reasons for the Liberals' success. First, the trade union-ists feared that Conservative policies such as those relating to Taff Vale, Chinese slavery, trade and social conditions would result in a worsening of working and living conditions, and therefore they voted for the Liberals or the LRC. Second, the middle classes also distrusted the Conservatives as a result of their handling of the Boer War and tariff reform. They believed the Liberals had put their problems behind them and were far more united over questions linked to trade, empire and Ireland. This was reinforced by the traditional nature of the election manifesto put forward by the Liberals. Finally, the Conservatives had experienced organisational difficulties, which resulted in a number of Liberals standing unopposed.

Some historians have argued that overall the election result was more a case of a Conservative defeat than a Liberal victory. Indeed, the Liberal resurgence was relatively short-lived, as by the beginning of the interwar period the party was once again heading for decline.

Conclusion

The significance of the Liberal election victory of 1906 was twofold. First, it showed that the public was mistrustful of the Conservative Party and unhappy about a number of policies that the party had adopted. Second, it signalled that the Liberal Party was still a political force to be reckoned with and could appeal to an expanding electorate. It also led to the Liberal welfare reforms and the roots of a welfare state.

How far was the First World War responsible for the growth of the Labour Party and the decline of the Liberal Party?

Summary

By 1923 the Labour Party had overturned the Liberals to become one of the two strongest political parties in Britain. You will need to examine the origins of the Labour Party and its relationship with the trade union movement. You will also need to study the significance of the First World War in determining the fortunes of all the major political groups. In particular there should be some focus on the debate over why the Liberal Party declined. Was it due simply to the 'rampant omnibus' of the war or were there longer-term factors of equal significance?

The Labour Representation Committee and the foundation of the Labour Party

The Labour Representation Committee (LRC) was formed in February 1900 by a mixture of members of various socialist societies (the **Socialist Democratic Federation**,

content guidance

Fabians, **Independent Labour Party**) and trade unions. According to **Keir Hardie**, a prominent figure in the Labour movement, the aim was to create an organisation that would form a 'distinct Labour group in Parliament', which had been sadly lacking. Prior to this, working men who had the vote could have given their support to Liberal, Conservative or independent Members of Parliament. There was increasing disenchantment with the two main parties, however, as they appeared to be making no headway in tackling some of the growing economic and social issues that affected working people: declining real wages, increasing unemployment and deteriorating living conditions, as revealed by the social surveys of Booth and Rowntree. Even the the Liberals' promise to push special Labour representation into Parliament (Lib-Labs) failed to impress. By 1900 only 11 such representatives existed.

The LRC was considered to be a 'socialistic' body. This meant that to unify all Labour groups there had to be a compromise between those who believed in the more radical ideas of socialism and those who were moderate, which still included substantial sections of the trade union movement. This was not an easy task, and as there were many factions that had to work closely together it was inevitable that it would be some time before a totally integrated Labour Party achieved political success.

The first major success for the LRC came in the general election of 1900 when two members, Keir Hardie and Richard Bell, were elected for Merthyr Tydfil and Derby respectively. In the years that followed, the LRC gained support rapidly, especially from trade union members. This was partly linked to the **Taff Vale judgement** of 1901, which meant that a union could be sued for damages resulting from strike action.

Many union members found this abhorrent and saw the LRC as the party that would best represent their interests in the future. In 1902 and 1903 the LRC won two by-elections and started to give cause for concern to the Liberals, who considered themselves the main party of the working class at the time. This resulted in an electoral pact being formed in 1903 between the Liberal representative, **Herbert Gladstone**, and the LRC secretary, **Ramsay MacDonald**. The Liberals agreed not to contest certain seats at general elections in return for LRC support within Parliament. This benefited the LRC enormously. In the general election of 1906, 29 members were successful. Further progress was slow, however, with the Labour vote never exceeding 7.6% nationally before the outbreak of the First World War.

The problem for the Labour Party before the war was that it was difficult to break away totally from the Liberals to provide its own distinguishable programme for reform. This was reinforced by the introduction of the Liberals' social reform programme dealing with issues relating to child welfare, the elderly, the unemployed and the sick, which was designed to appeal to the masses.

The influence of trade unions

By 1900 the nature of trade unionism had changed considerably with the emergence of '**general unionism**'. General unions catered for all types of worker and were more prepared to take direct action to achieve the basic aims of higher wages and reduced hours of work. The use of the strike and picketing was commonplace, but was curtailed by the Taff Vale judgement. This was upheld by the House of Lords during a period of Conservative Party rule, although the Liberals seemed just as keen to side with employers during industrial disputes. The significance of this was that unions increasingly looked for representation from an independent Labour Party. The decision by the Lords resulted in 127 unions affiliating with the LRC, which increased membership from 353,000 in 1900 to 847,000 by 1903.

There was something of a lull in union activity up to 1906 but subsequently membership numbers started to rise significantly. There was a dramatic increase after 1910, which coincided with considerable industrial unrest. In 1912, the 'crisis' year, over a million trade unionists were involved in 857 strikes, including the first national coal-miners' strike. Employers took a hard line and the authorities were prepared to use force in the form of troops to keep law and order.

For the Labour Party the consequences of this burst of activity were twofold. First, in theory, more trade unionists meant more finance, although this process was adversely affected by the **Osborne judgement** of 1909, which said that unions could not force members to pay a subscription to a political party. The problem was slightly eased by the introduction of payment for MPs in 1911, although the Osborne judgement was not reversed until 1913, with the passing of the Trade Union Act. Second, union militancy, especially as it was associated with the radical views of **syndicalism** at the time, appeared to weaken the credibility of the Labour Party in Parliament.

Despite opposition, trade unions had reached a period of considerable strength by 1914. Many unskilled workers had been unionised and separate unions were working together — as characterised by the Triple Alliance (railwaymen, miners and transport workers) of 1914 — to achieve common goals.

The suffragettes

In 1903 **Emmeline Pankhurst** founded the **Women's Social and Political Union**, which campaigned for votes for women and formed the basis of the suffragette movement. Pankhurst had been a member of the Independent Labour Party (ILP), but had become totally disillusioned with its negative attitude towards female suffrage. In fact, the Labour view was identical to that of the Liberals and Conservatives, and it was not until 1912, after much militant campaigning and pressure, that the Labour Party conference accepted a female suffrage resolution. Some women were granted the vote for the first time in 1918 and this was undoubtedly influenced by the role they had played during the war. The majority of Labour and Liberal party members had generally been against this before 1914 and, with hindsight, had not handled the suffrage issue very effectively.

The impact of the First World War domestic politics

The Labour movement benefited from the war as the demand for workers exceeded supply, which 'naturally' forced wages up and put unions in a strong bargaining position. Subsequently, union membership increased further from around 4 million in 1914 to 6 million in 1918. The Labour Party also became stronger as a result of its direct involvement in governing the country as part of a coalition government from 1915 to 1917. In 1917, however, Labour cabinet member, **Arthur Henderson**, was forced to resign, which resulted in the ending of the Lib-Lab pact and the re-forming of Labour into a better-organised and fully independent body.

The Liberals, on the other hand, were adversely affected as they disagreed over how the war should be run. **Herbert Asquith**, the Liberal prime minister at the outbreak of the war, and his secretary of state for war, Lord Kitchener, failed to inspire confidence as a crisis emerged over the supplying of munitions and reports of very heavy casualties. In December 1916 Asquith was replaced by **David Lloyd George** as leader of the wartime coalition government, which effectively meant the Liberals were split into two camps. Asquith and all of his supporters failed to gain a place in the new government, although they vowed to support it. A feud developed with Lloyd George, which continued well after the end of the war.

The condition of the political parties at the end of the war

A general election was held a month after the Armistice was signed. It was conducted under the influence of the **Representation of the People Act** (1918), which gave the vote to men over the age of 21 and women over 30. This increased the number of voters from 8 million to just under 22 million. Lloyd George and his Conservative ally, **Andrew Bonar Law**, pushed for the preservation of a coalition government and issued signed letters of endorsement for candidates who wished to follow them. Asquith mockingly called the endorsements 'coupons' and the election became known as the **Coupon Election**. The majority of the new electorate voted for members of parties that made up the coalition, providing it with 526 seats in Parliament. The opposition parties gained 181 seats.

The Conservatives gained most from the 1918 election and were by far the strongest party in the coalition. They had thrived on the divisions within the Liberal Party and the abandonment by Labour of the Lib-Lab pact. The Labour Party in opposition did well to gain 57 seats, although these were fewer than Sinn Fein, with 73. The Liberals were in disarray and within 4 years declined to become the 'third' political party in Britain.

Conclusion

The First World War was responsible for the growth of the Labour Party for the following reasons:
- There was full employment, which placed trade unions in a strong position.
- Members of the party had experience of governing the country.
- The party disassociated itself from the coalition, particularly the Liberals, to form a distinct party for the working class. (You should remember, however, that the seeds of growth had been planted long before the war. The decline of the Liberal Party may have been hastened by the war.)

- There was a split between Asquith and his supporters and Lloyd George and his supporters.
- The alliance with the Liberals broke up.

The roots of the Liberals' decline, though, were probably more deep-seated. A key point is that, despite the Liberal welfare reforms, many voters were still sceptical about the ability of the Liberals to cater for the wants and needs of the whole nation.

To what extent was a modern welfare state created by the Liberals between 1906 and 1914?

Summary

The origins of Liberal social reforms can be traced back to the end of the nineteenth century, although there was little evidence of the pre-planned programme in the party and candidate manifestos issued before the 1906 election. When considering the reforms, bear in mind the following:
- The reforms can be viewed as a package with a general set of influences.
- There were also specific reasons for the carrying out of individual measures.
- 'Modern welfare state' implies the optimum form of provision for everyone in society.
- It may be better to consider the reforms as a minimum form of provision catering for a range of citizens.

This will help you provide a balanced evaluation of the key issues.

The aims and extent of the Liberals' social reforms from 1906 to 1914

There were two general aims behind the Liberals' social reforms:
- The Liberals wanted to gain the support of the working classes and, in connection with this, to lessen the threat of socialism. This influence can be seen in the passing of measures relating to children and the elderly.
- They aimed to create a more efficient nation that would continue to hold on to its status as the major world power. This was especially important at a time when there was increased economic competition from Germany and the USA, and various social surveys had indicated that the health of the British was declining. The low fitness level of potential recruits for the Second Boer War (1899–1902) and rising infant mortality reinforced the view that Britain was in a poor state and was certainly not in a position to rule over an empire. Concerns over national efficiency were clearly reflected in legislation relating to health and employment.

The social reforms came in two phases: the first during the premiership of **Henry Campbell-Bannerman** (1906–08); the second during that of Herbert Asquith (1908–16). Key reforms in the first period were as follows:

- There were attempts to improve the health and welfare of children through the introduction of **school meals** (1906), **medical inspection** (1907) and the **Children's Act** (1908), which banned the imprisonment of children under 14 and made parents more responsible for the behaviour of their offspring.
- The **Old Age Pensions Act** (1908) was passed, which enabled people over 70 to claim a single rate of 5 shillings per week (25p) where their incomes were less than £26 per annum.

These reforms had a mixed level of success. By the beginning of the First World War only half of the education authorities were providing school meals for about 30,000 children, and about three-quarters were supplying facilities for medical treatment. Although pensions removed the stigma attached to poor law relief, they were not particularly generous and did not cover all the elderly. They were very well received by the general public, however.

The second phase of the reforms was characterised by the following:

- The **Labour Exchanges Act** (1909) looked to solve the problem of underemployment by improving awareness of job vacancies for workers.
- The **Trade Boards Act** (1909) aimed to improve wages and working conditions for the notorious 'sweated trades'.
- **National Insurance**, against unemployment and ill-health, was introduced in 1911. Unemployment insurance was to cover those in selected trades prone to cyclical or seasonal unemployment. Health insurance covered all workers earning less than £160 per annum and they would receive weekly sickness benefit and free medical treatment. Both schemes involved employers, employees and the state making contributions. National Insurance is a prime example of where there had been specific influences for reform. It was based partly on the findings of the 1909 **Royal Commission on the Poor Law** and, more significantly, on the German model for insurance, which had been investigated by the chancellor of the exchequer, Lloyd George.

Again there were critics of these reforms who pointed out the limited benefits on offer, the fact that substantial contributions had to be made and that women and the children of breadwinners were not covered. There was also concern about infringement of the rights of individuals to choose. However, the reforms were a major success for Asquith and the rising stars in his cabinet, Winston Churchill and Lloyd George.

The role of Lloyd George

David Lloyd George entered Campbell-Bannerman's cabinet as president of the Board of Trade. In this role he was responsible for the passing of the **Merchant Shipping Act** (1906), the first **census of industrial production** (1907), the establishment of the **Port of London Authority** (1908) and the settlement of a number of difficult industrial disputes. Initially, there had been some concern that the Welshman was full of words and ideas but would be unable to put them into practice. He proved his critics wrong with his energy, vision and considerable administrative and political skill.

Lloyd George's ability led to promotion under Asquith to the post of chancellor of the exchequer. His immediate task was to calculate how old age pensions and the construction of Dreadnought battleships could be financed. The result was the far-reaching '**People's Budget**' of 1909, which was quickly followed by a major constitutional crisis involving the House of Lords.

The struggles with the House of Lords

Lloyd George had little time for those in society who gained wealth from land ownership. Thus, the 1909 budget took money from the rich to give to the poor through a series of taxation measures, which included a super-tax on those earning more than £5,000 per annum and various land taxes. The Lords were infuriated and refused to agree to these measures. Asquith was forced to call a general election in January 1910 in an attempt to gain the support of the nation. The Liberals were returned with a clear majority of 124 and the budget was eventually passed on 28 April 1910.

To prevent a repeat of this, Asquith looked to pass a **Parliament Act**, which would severely limit the power of Lords. With the threat of the creation of hundreds of new peers and the backing of the electorate through another general election victory in December 1910, the Parliament Bill became law in August 1911. The Lords could no longer veto a finance bill and were left only with powers of delay in other matters. Asquith and Lloyd George had won a major victory.

Conclusion

It would be an exaggeration to say that a modern welfare state had been created by the Liberals between 1906 and 1914. Despite the emergence, to an extent, of 'new liberalism', it would have been unthinkable for any government at the time to have intervened fully in the lives of all citizens to improve their welfare. There was still much support for individualism and a *laissez-faire* approach to welfare as the basis of economic and social progress. Hence the reforms were limited in scope and nature.

The reforms did, however, show a willingness for greater state intervention. This had a positive effect on millions of citizens who previously could only have turned to the stigmatised Poor Law or specialised private institutions, such as friendly societies, for help. To this extent a kind of social services state was created, which laid the foundations for a fully integrated welfare state.

How serious was the crisis in England over the issue of Ireland from 1909 to 1916?

Summary

The key Irish issue during this period was still **Home Rule**. You will need to know about Asquith's attitude towards Home Rule, the 1912 Home Rule Bill and the response from **Irish nationalists** and those living in Ulster. The main focus should be on understanding how this impacted upon politics in England.

Attitudes to Ireland in England

The year 1909 is significant in that it witnessed the presentation of the 'People's Budget', which led to a constitutional crisis over the role of the House of Lords. Asquith had been appointed prime minister in 1908 and took a more positive, reforming stance than his predecessors. To pay for social reforms, such as old age pensions, a radical budget was introduced. It aimed to redistribute wealth from the very rich to the poor and, needless to say, was opposed by the landed classes. In response, Asquith decided to dissolve Parliament and call a general election on the issues of the budget, the House of Lords and free trade. The Liberals won, but only just, and found that the Irish nationalists, with 82 seats, held the balance of power. Their leader, **John Redmond**, saw an opportunity to do a deal. He pushed Asquith to make a commitment to introduce Home Rule in exchange for the support of the nationalists in Parliament. It could be argued that Asquith had no option but to agree, although there is evidence to suggest that he had some sympathy for the nationalist movement.

The attitude of the Conservatives to Home Rule had not really changed since the time of Balfour. It was to be opposed, although support for the Irish 'peasantry' should continue, as provided by the 1903 **Land Purchase Act**. Thus, attitudes to Ireland in England at this time were polarised between those who were for and those who were against Home Rule. This polarisation was strengthened by events that occurred after 1911.

The 1912 Home Rule Bill

Asquith personally introduced the **Third Home Rule Bill** in April 1912. It was not dissimilar to the Home Rule Bill of 1893, with an emphasis on ultimate rule from Westminster with Ireland having a separate government to rule over internal matters. There was still considerable opposition, however. The most prosperous areas of Ireland were located in the Ulster region of the industrialised north. Industrial growth had been mainly a result of British capital and expertise, and subsequently most of

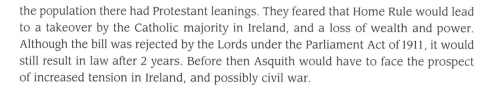

the population there had Protestant leanings. They feared that Home Rule would lead to a takeover by the Catholic majority in Ireland, and a loss of wealth and power. Although the bill was rejected by the Lords under the Parliament Act of 1911, it would still result in law after 2 years. Before then Asquith would have to face the prospect of increased tension in Ireland, and possibly civil war.

Ulster resistance

The Ulster Party, led by **Sir James Craig**, had already started to bargain with Asquith over Home Rule before the bill was introduced. Members of this party hoped Ulster could remain independent, with a separate provisional government. To reinforce their case they formed an alliance with Bonar Law and the Conservatives and started to form their own mini army, the **Ulster Volunteers** (Ulster Volunteer Force or UVF). Asquith took no action and adopted a '**wait-and-see**' approach.

For 2 years the Ulster Volunteers became increasingly organised and built up support. Early in 1914 they were given something of a boost when army officers based in Carragh, Dublin, voted to accept dismissal from their post rather than agree to take up arms against the people of Ulster. Although this was resolved with guarantees that they would not be asked to do so, it caused controversy as there was some suspicion that the Conservatives had prompted the mutiny. Another cause for concern was the gun-carrying operation carried out by the UVF in April 1914. A substantial number of rifles and ammunition were obtained, which gave further impetus to the growth of a nationalist army.

The Irish nationalists

An Irish nationalist army (the **Irish Volunteers**) was formed in response to the UVF, from 1913 to 1914. A compromise of sorts was reached in March 1914, when parliamentary parties agreed that Ulster should be allowed to take a vote on whether to be excluded from Home Rule for a period of 6 years. But this did not prove acceptable to the nationalists or Ulstermen, although it had become almost impossible to suspend Home Rule.

The Home Rule Act was passed in September 1914, but as Britain was at war with Germany, the provisions of the act were suspended. This was accepted by Redmond, but annoyed the increasingly influential nationalist organisation, **Sinn Fein**. Redmond believed the war would soon end and Home Rule would be in place, but he was proved wrong. As the war dragged on, the nationalist influence waned, particularly after the formation of a coalition government. The more revolutionary nationalists gained increasing support for their antiwar stance and this led to a major crisis in 1916.

The Easter rebellion, 1916

By the end of 1914 the Irish Volunteers were divided between a majority, who followed Redmond's call to support the war effort through active service (the National

Volunteers), and a minority (the Irish Volunteers), who opposed the war. The leader of the dissidents was **Eoin MacNeill**, but there were other, more militant extremists who wished to take their opposition further. An armed rebellion was planned to take place at Easter 1916, starting in Dublin. When the plans were put into operation there was little resistance and the rebels easily established a headquarters at the general post office in the city centre. The authorities were taken by surprise, but by Easter Monday they had gained the upper hand, and within a week the uprising had been suppressed.

The perpetrators of the revolt were harshly dealt with by the British authorities, which only helped reunite the nationalist factions. This caused Asquith to reassess the situation and he appointed Lloyd George to negotiate a quick settlement between Redmond and Sir Edward Carson, leader of the Irish Unionists. But powerful unionists in the coalition government continued to oppose an immediate introduction of Home Rule. This resulted in a rapid decline in the authority of Redmond and paved the way for Sinn Fein to take the place of his parliamentary party.

Conclusion

From 1909 to 1916 Irish issues were of considerable concern in England due to:
- Liberal reliance on Irish nationalist support after the 1910 general elections
- the debate over the Home Rule Act of 1914
- worries over the growth of Irish nationalist and unionist armies
- the support given by the Conservatives to the unionists
- the possibility of civil war in Ireland
- the distraction caused during the first 2 years of the First World War

Despite this, Asquith remained rather detached from Irish issues. Understandably, during the war his main concerns had been maintaining government unity and his own position as prime minister.

Interwar domestic problems, 1918–39

The four key issues for study and examination are:
(1) Why did Lloyd George win so overwhelmingly in the 1918 election, yet fall from power in 1922?
(2) What were the causes and significance of the General Strike of 1926?
(3) How effective were the Labour governments of 1924 and 1929–31?
(4) How successfully did the National Governments of 1931–39 deal with their problems?

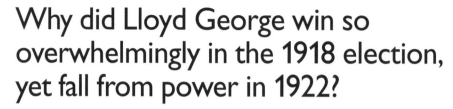

Why did Lloyd George win so overwhelmingly in the 1918 election, yet fall from power in 1922?

Summary

Lloyd George was considered to be the 'man who won the war'. He vowed to 'reconstruct' the economy and society after the war with promises of improving living standards. Within 4 years, however, he had fallen from power. To explain this change in fortune you will need to consider the personality of Lloyd George, the Liberal Party split, factors that weakened the coalition government, and the changing economic and social context of the early postwar period.

The domestic problems faced by Lloyd George's government, 1918–22

Lloyd George's re-elected coalition government of 1918 faced a range of economic, social and political problems. Returning troops and displaced civilian wartime workers, including many women, had to be supported while they tried to find suitable work. This transitory unemployment was partly dealt with through the use of '**out-of-work donations**', but by 1921 there were the first signs that unemployment might be of a more long-term, cyclical nature. This was to be exacerbated by the fact that overseas markets had been lost during the war and there had been a general lack of investment in industry, much of which had been temporarily nationalised. Wartime loans would also have to be paid back. All this started to contribute to an economic crisis with which Lloyd George found it difficult to deal.

Three major social issues existed at the end of the war: housing, education and health. Lloyd George had promised '**homes fit for heroes**', and widening access to education at various levels had been planned through Fisher's **Education Act** of 1918. By 1922 nearly all of the plans for social reform had been put on hold and were restricted by the '**Geddes axe**', a package of drastic public expenditure cuts.

There were also political difficulties for Lloyd George as his own party was split between his followers and the so-called '**Squiffites**', supporters of Asquith. Lloyd George's coalition government was dependent on a Conservative majority and there was considerable opposition from a strengthened Labour Party. Tense industrial relations continued after the war and there was still the unresolved problem of Ireland.

The Liberal splits

During the first 2 years of the war Asquith was criticised for his lack of ability to plan and show a sense of urgency in his decision-making. He was blamed for early military defeats and the munitions or '**shells crisis**'. He also opposed conscription, which he believed ran against traditional Liberal values. Asquith managed to counter some of the criticism by forming a coalition government with the help of Bonar Law, the Conservative leader. But by December 1916 Lloyd George had colluded with Bonar Law and the Labour leader, Arthur Henderson, to form a streamlined war cabinet, which would exclude Asquith. About half the Liberal Party sided with Asquith, whom they saw as the bastion of traditional Liberalism. The split was eventually healed, but not before severe damage had been done to the Liberals' chances of ever again being elected to run the country.

The 'Coupon Election' of 1918 proved to be a victory for the electoral pact formed between Lloyd George and Bonar Law. By the next election of 1922 the Liberals were still divided between National or Coalition Liberals and more traditional Liberals. Coupled with the fact that there had been mounting concern over how Lloyd George was tackling the economic problems of the 1920s, the result of the election was a clear victory for the Conservatives, who no longer saw the need for Liberal support. More significant was the success of Labour, which overtook the combined total of Liberal seats.

It could be argued that the Liberal splits can be traced back to the second half of the nineteenth century. There were those who wished to remain true to the traditional values of the Liberal Party and those who saw a need to move with the times and create a 'new' liberalism, which would, in particular, appeal to the expanding working-class electorate and lessen the threat of a rising Labour Party. This would make the First World War the occasion for, rather than the cause of, the last Liberal government.

The breakdown in the coalition

Lloyd George led a coalition government dependent on a Conservative majority. He was supported by Bonar Law, and later by **Austen Chamberlain**, but other Conservatives were far more suspicious of his motives and viewed him as unpredictable. Despite early success with social reforms and solving industrial disputes, there was mounting Conservative backbench resentment. This was due to:

- Lloyd George agreeing to the creation of an Irish Free State, which left unionists feeling betrayed
- the maintenance of high taxation and what was considered to be wastefulness in public expenditure (especially with respect to Christopher Addison's new housing scheme)
- the sale of honours (knighthoods etc.) to increase the Liberal funds
- the loss of by-elections to Labour
- Lloyd George's association with a 'soft' appeasement-based policy towards postwar Germany

Lloyd George maintained the support of senior Conservatives up to the end of 1922 and pushed for an election to re-establish his control. Backbench pressure proved too great and the idea of a coalition being carried forward was rejected. On 19 October 1922 Lloyd George resigned.

The reasons for Lloyd George's fall

Lloyd George's eventual fall from power was partly a result of his personality. He was a highly energetic, lively politician, who was keen to see ideas implemented quickly to achieve effective results. This often involved bypassing certain rules and regulations. He was also considered to be self-centred, over-ambitious and unwilling to cooperate fully as part of a team. On occasion he used people, as with Addison, and broke promises to save his own neck. As Minister of Reconstruction, Addison made a brave attempt to meet Lloyd George's housing targets under difficult circumstances. He was still accused of producing too little at too high a cost and became a scapegoat for the failure to fulfil the 'homes fit for heroes' promise. All of this alienated Lloyd George from fellow politicians, although there were many who gave their loyal support.

As we have already seen, Lloyd George's fortunes were also dented by his falling out with Asquith, the revolt of the Conservative backbenchers and the strengthening of the Labour Party. In addition, the economic problems of the early 1920s were not something over which he had much control and the expenditure cuts were in line with orthodox thinking at the time.

Summary

Lloyd George won so overwhelmingly in the 1918 election due to:
- his association with winning the war
- his promise to 'reconstruct' the economy and society

He fell from power in 1922 as he:
- personally alienated potential supporters
- was part of a divided Liberal Party
- failed to hold together a Conservative-dominated coalition
- could not fend off Labour Party opposition
- was a victim of changing economic circumstances

What were the causes and significance of the General Strike of 1926?

Summary

The term 'general strike' is rather misleading as the events of 1926 constituted a sympathy strike in support of the miners. Even then, not all workers went on strike and there was much regional variation in the extent and impact of the event. You should understand the long-term, short-term and 'trigger' causes of the strike. With respect to its significance, make sure that you focus on the economic and political consequences before 1939.

The economic situation after the First World War

British politicians faced a number of economic problems at the end of the First World War. These related to the labour force, lost capital, lost markets and the availability of capital.

- Over three-quarters of a million men were killed during the war, with a further 1.5 million injured. This created a qualitative, as well as a quantitative, loss for the labour force, although this was compensated to a large extent by the entry of women into the labour market for the first time.
- Much fixed capital was lost, including two-fifths of the merchant shipping fleet. There was a general lack of investment in updating and replacing old machinery, including in mining.
- The war was a great drain financially. Estimates suggest that the cost for Britain was £9,000 million. This was met by the sale of overseas assets, borrowing (largely from the USA) and the raising of taxes. Loans were also made to Allies and, in the case of Russia, proved impossible to retrieve in full.
- Overseas markets were lost to economic rivals such as the USA.

All of these factors were to contribute to the economic depressions that had a devastating effect in the interwar period.

Labour unrest

The Labour movement continued to be in a strong position after the war. Membership grew, as did the number of strikes. In 1918, 6 million working days were lost to strike action but by 1921 this had risen to 85 million.

The coalition government proved fairly successful in dealing with some of the major incidents, such as the 9-day rail strike of 1919 and the dockers' dispute of 1920. Its major triumph was the handling of the 1921 miners' dispute, which, through the use of delay tactics, resulted in the **Miners' Federation** being divided from its allies in the transport unions. The miners eventually backed down, which resulted in a strengthening of the position of employers and a weakening of the Labour Party. The problems of the mining industry and the other 'old staple' industries did not go away, however, and by the mid-1920s there were further attempts to reduce wages and generally worsen working conditions.

The causes of the 1926 General Strike

There were long-term, short-term and immediate factors that resulted in the General Strike of 1926. Note the following:

- The strike was called by the **Trades Union Congress** (TUC) in support of the miners who had been 'locked out' by their employers. The miners had been refused entry into work by the mine-owners in response to the threat of industrial action.
- The mining industry had always been fraught with difficulties. Since it began to expand in the 1830s it was characterised by concerns over safety, hours of work, wage levels of miners, investment in new technology and competition from abroad. Generally, it was an old staple industry that struggled to improve efficiency.

As these problems proved increasingly difficult to resolve, tensions between employers and employees grew. By the end of the First World War a powerful miners' union had been formed and started to demand higher wages, fewer hours and nationalisation of the industry. The **Sankey Commission** of 1919 responded positively to these requests, but the trade depression of 1920 resulted in mine owners pushing for wage cuts to be made. In turn, the Miners' Federation reacted through the **triple alliance** with railway and transport workers (formed in 1914) to threaten industrial action. On 31 March 1921 the miners were locked out but within 2 weeks had lost the support of the other unions, which strengthened the position of employers. It also left a feeling of bitterness amongst the miners.

- During the year before the General Strike a number of events once again brought the problem of the miners to the fore. There had been a substantial increase in the European demand for coal, partly due to France's occupation of the Ruhr coal-mining area in Germany. But Britain's return to the Gold Standard in April 1925 prompted a rise in the value of the pound and over-priced British exports. By the summer of 1925 mine owners were once again claiming the need for wages to be decreased and hours to go up — otherwise workers would be laid off. Initially, **Stanley Baldwin**, the Conservative leader, backed the employers, but on 31 July 1925 (**Red Friday**) he agreed to subsidise miners' wages while an investigation was carried out. This was known as the **Samuel Commission** and reported in March 1926. It offered a compromise solution and was generally sympathetic towards the miners, although it stated that they should accept wage reductions. The miners' leader, **A. J. Cook**, responded with the famous claim that there would be 'not a penny off the pay, not a minute on the day' and the mine owners also flatly rejected the recommendations of the commission. A deadlock in negotiations occurred, worsened by the ending of wage subsidies on 30 April. On 1 May 1926 the mine owners once again 'locked out' the miners.

- The immediate cause of the General Strike was the call for support by the TUC from selected groups of strategic workers. They would stop work on 4 May, although negotiations would continue up until then. Following a disagreement between printers and employers at the *Daily Mail* newspaper over the reporting of the dispute, Baldwin announced that there would be no more discussions. He was confident of a positive outcome for employers, as the government had made a rigorous effort to plan against the potential disruption of a general strike. From 4–12 May 1926 the General Strike proceeded, with limited but solid support for the miners.

The consequences of the 1926 General Strike

There were immediate and longer-term consequences of the strike:

- The TUC had not planned effectively for the strike, but the government was extremely well organised. In addition, there were moderates within the TUC who were worried about the claim that they were acting 'unconstitutionally' and that the protest had a 'revolutionary' flavour to it. Thus, the TUC leadership was pushed into abandoning the strike on 12 May without obtaining any concessions.

The miners struggled on until November 1926, when they were forced, through increasing poverty, to return to work under worsened conditions of service.

- The strike left the Labour movement divided, trade unions in debt and a fall in union membership. Overall, it was a humiliating experience.
- In 1927 a **Trade Disputes and Trade Union Act** was passed, which placed severe restrictions on union activity with the aim of preventing further national disputes. This was not repealed until 1946.

Conclusion

The causes of the strike were linked with:

- problems faced by the mining industry that dated back to the nineteenth century
- the increasing power of the miners' union and the TUC
- the uncompromising nature of the mine owners
- Baldwin's support for the mine owners

The strike resulted in:

- a moral victory for the mine owners and the government
- a divided Labour movement
- general concern about the possibility of revolution
- legislation that hindered union activity

How effective were the Labour governments of 1924 and 1929–31?

Summary

The effectiveness of the Labour governments of this period can be measured by looking at the extent to which their aims were achieved. You will also need to consider the context within which the Labour governments were operating. Both governments were in a minority position and that of 1929–31 was unlucky enough to experience the knock-on effects of the 1929 **Wall Street Crash** in the USA. It is also important to assess the role of the Labour leader, **Ramsay MacDonald**, as there is much controversy over how he conducted affairs, particularly from 1929 to 1931.

The aims, characteristics and problems of the Labour governments of 1924 and 1929–31

The first ever Labour government was appointed in January 1924. In the preceding general election of December 1923 Labour had gained 191 seats, the Liberals 159 and the Conservatives a substantial 258. Together Labour and the Liberals were in a position to outvote the Conservatives in Parliament over a range of issues. Probably the most contentious subject of the time was trade policy. Both the Liberals and Labour favoured free trade, whereas the Conservatives had protectionist ideas. Labour, as the strongest free-trade party, was therefore asked to take office. The Labour government

elected in May 1929 won 287 seats, the Conservatives 260 and the Liberals 59, which again resulted in a minority administration.

In many ways the aims and characteristics of both governments were similar. They were also not very different from those of their political rivals:

- **Economic aims:** Labour attempted to stabilise the economy by restricting expenditure and maintaining a balanced budget. This was known as retrenchment. It eventually became a major reason for a split in the party in 1931 when **Snowden**, the chancellor of the exchequer, decided to reduce unemployment benefit.
- **Social aims:** both governments sought to alleviate poverty caused by unemployment, old age and sickness. The 1924 government showed a particular interest in living conditions and passed the **Wheatley Housing Act**, which subsidised the building of council housing for rent.
- **Political aims:** as the Labour Party formed minority governments the leadership argued the need to adopt a cautious approach domestically and was aware of the reliance on the Liberals for support. In foreign affairs there was much continuity during both administrations, with a commitment to the maintenance of empire and emphasis on creating stability within Europe through the reconciliation of Germany.

Generally, the Labour governments were characterised by moderation, conservatism and a willingness to cooperate with the institutions of capitalism. For many Labour politicians this went against what the party was meant to stand for. There were those who wanted a revolutionary change of society based on genuine socialist policies. Thus, another characteristic was the distance that the leadership created between themselves and the more committed socialist party members.

Both Labour governments faced a range of problems. In 1924 there was much debate over what the party stood for, with the famous **Clause Four** of its constitution being interpreted differently by different people. This was a statement added to the constitution in 1918 which committed the party to a socialist policy of obtaining '...the common ownership of the means of production'. Trade unions were very influential in dictating party policy, which also caused public concern. The party's greatest problem, however, was that it seemed to be associated with communism. This was reinforced, firstly by MacDonald's refusal to proceed with a prosecution against **J. R. Campbell**, the editor of a left-wing newspaper accused of publishing subversive material. This was followed by the **Zinoviev** affair, in which the *Daily Mail* published a letter, supposedly written by an important member of the government of Soviet Russia, urging the Communist Party of Britain to start a revolution. The Conservatives linked this to the Labour Party as part of its '**red scare**' tactics. In the general election of October 1924 Labour lost 40 seats, letting the Conservatives back into power. It is unclear how much this was due to the 'red scare' policy, however, as there had been a more significant loss of votes and seats by the Liberals.

The biggest problem for the second Labour government was dealing with the effects of the 1929 Wall Street Crash. Within a year of coming into office unemployment had risen to over 2 million; this was linked with a dramatic decline in trade. MacDonald seemed to lack vision over how to deal with the problem and continued with an orthodox approach, which culminated in severe cutbacks in government expenditure in 1931. MacDonald supported his chancellor, Snowden, in making a 10% reduction in unemployment benefit, which seemed to go against Labour principles. This divided both the party and government, and in August 1931 MacDonald resigned.

The leadership of Ramsay MacDonald

During both periods of Labour government it was clear that MacDonald had little time for the more 'left-wing' members of the party. He wanted to bring 'respectability' to the Labour movement and to create a party that was accessible to all social classes. The 1924 government was obviously an attempt to show that there was nothing to fear about Labour and that it was fit to govern. This was reflected in the make-up of the cabinet, which contained many orthodox thinkers and only one radical, Wheatley. This trend continued with the 1929 government. Snowden, for example, was again chancellor, but his policies hardly seemed different from those of the Conservatives and the Liberals.

MacDonald is viewed by many historians as incompetent, devious, lacking in tact and out of his depth. After the cuts of 1931 he was labelled as a traitor to his party and the working class, and this was reinforced when he agreed to head a Conservative-dominated coalition government during the early 1930s. Maybe this is rather an unfair judgement, as MacDonald faced unprecedented economic problems and, at times, had a genuine desire to see Labour as the second force in British politics.

The adoption of a National Government

When MacDonald resigned as prime minister in August 1931 he was immediately asked by the king to form a coalition government. This National Government, as it became known, was considered to be an extraordinary measure to deal with the extraordinary problem of unemployment, which had continued to rise to 3 million by the end of 1931. It was supported by the majority of Conservatives, Liberals, and Labour supporters of MacDonald. Other Labour Party members were astounded and believed that MacDonald had connived to gain himself a position of power and status. Subsequently, MacDonald was expelled from the Labour Party in September 1931 and a hard core of party members went on to oppose the policies of the National Government.

Conclusion

To an extent both Labour governments were effective in that they stuck to their aims. The first government showed particular promise in the field of social policy, with its housing legislation. But the governments were not effective in so far as they failed to cope with the economic problems of the time, which was a main reason for the split in 1931. MacDonald was inconsistent as prime minister and must take some blame for a lack of achievement, but above all it must be remembered that the governments were also victims of circumstances that were beyond their control.

How successfully did the National Governments of 1931–39 deal with their problems?

Summary

With this key issue you are expected to focus on the economic problems faced by the National Governments. There was some success in dealing with these once the governments started to move away from traditional, orthodox policies. There were, however, other factors that enabled the British economy to revive, such as the growth of new industries and rising consumer expenditure. The latter was reflected in a number of social developments, such as the use of the motorcar and cinema-going.

The economic problems of the 1930s

The crash of the stock market in New York in 1929 had serious repercussions for western European economies. By 1931 an economic depression hit Britain and a National (coalition) Government, headed by Ramsay MacDonald, was set up to deal with the problem.

The main issue was unemployment, which by the early months of 1932 had reached 3 million. There was a steady decline after this so that by 1939 the number was around 1.5 million, although the pattern had been temporarily reversed in 1937–38. Unemployment acted as an indicator to governments of how well the economy was operating, but it also posed social problems that had to be confronted. With hindsight, it is clear that high and persistent unemployment in the 1930s was due to a number of causes and was not simply the result of a slump in trade. There were also structural problems with British industry, particularly the old staples (coal, textiles, iron and steel), which meant that they struggled to compete with foreign counterparts. It can be argued that the National Governments did not fully understand the complexity of the unemployment issue and therefore adopted policies that may not have been appropriate.

The policies of the National Governments

The 1931–35 National Government focused on attempting to revive British trading prospects while assuming that the free market would eventually balance out, leading to a 'natural' decline in unemployment. Crucial to this was the maintenance of a balanced budget, which resulted in retrenchment or expenditure cuts. These were very controversial and even at the time there were those who claimed it would exacerbate the situation. The government believed that less expenditure equalled less inflation, which in turn meant that British goods could be sold abroad cheaper. This was aided by a devaluation of the pound in 1931. The lowering of interest rates to 2% in 1932 was designed to stimulate private enterprise, and the reintroduction of import duties also

guidance

aimed to protect British industry. By the mid-1930s there was an acknowl[e] that some regions were far more depressed than others. The **Special Areas A** provided £2 million in aid to targeted areas to encourage labour mobility and [

The policies of the National Governments were of a fairly orthodox nature, however, and it is unclear whether they had any role in aiding the economic recovery that occurred after 1932. There is certainly no evidence to suggest they had a detrimental effect. It is more likely that improvement was a result of the growth of new industries, a housing boom, rising consumer expenditure and rearmament. New industries, such as the motor vehicle, chemical and electricity industries, undoubtedly contributed to rising industrial production and employment as a whole, but they were located mainly in the south and the Midlands.

The housing boom, instigated by a series of government acts, resulted in the creation of jobs and stimulated allied industries, such as brick-making and electricity. The motor vehicle industry also grew, resulting in the creation of more work, with about 400,000 people employed by 1939. Finally, from 1935 to 1939 the rearmament programme embarked upon by the government involved 1 million more people being employed.

Alternative solutions

The main alternative to orthodox thinking was based on the ideas of the economist **John Maynard Keynes**. He argued that rather than cut back on expenditure, governments should actually borrow money and spend it during times of economic depression to stimulate the overall level of demand in the economy. This could be achieved by creating public works such as roads, hospitals and schools. Such projects would create employment, and income earned would then be spent on consumer items, which would in turn create more demand and therefore more jobs. For many politicians this was an alien concept, although some Liberals and members of **Oswald Mosley's British Union of Fascists** saw merit in the theory. Thus, Keynesian views were rejected. Although some historians have pointed out that these ideas may not have been significant, Keynesian-type policies could have led to inflation, which would have made the depression worse.

Social change

There are a number of indicators which suggest that, despite economic depression in some regions, there was a considerable rise in living standards in others. This was again connected with the growth of new industries. As new areas of industrial activity arose, so did a range of services that reflected a more 'modern age'. Some related to work and others to leisure, particularly the radio, cinema and motorcar:

- **Radio:** radio broadcasts by the BBC had started in 1922 and by 1939 radios were owned by most householders. About 9 million licences had been issued by the end of the period, allowing listeners to tune in to programmes focusing mainly on news and music.

- **Cinema:** cinemas had spread throughout the 1920s but 1929 was a turning-point, with the introduction of 'talkies'. By 1939 there were nearly 5,000 cinemas screening a range of films to all classes in society.
- **Motorcar:** in 1939 it was estimated that there were about 3 million cars on the road. This was mainly the result of falling car prices. The Austin, Morris and Ford firms all attempted to construct some vehicles for around £100, which placed them within the budget of many working-class families.

There were other significant social trends, such as an increase in the reading of books and newspapers, more attendance at a variety of sporting events, gambling on the pools, and the spread of Woolworths and Marks & Spencer stores, which were indicative of greater affluence. There was a marked contrast in the country during the 1930s between the wealthier south and the struggling north. On the whole, the policies of the National Governments had little impact on narrowing the gap.

Conclusion

The National Governments of 1931–39 were successful in so far as:
- unemployment gradually decreased
- trade picked up
- inflation remained relatively low
- standards of living rose

These trends may not have been due to government policies, however, as:
- orthodox approaches were used to deal with trade cycle and market problems
- new industries emerged 'naturally' without government intervention to create wealth
- rearmament, an eventual necessity, created work

Foreign policy, 1939–63

The four key issues for study and examination are:
(1) How did the Second World War change the direction of British foreign policy?
(2) How and why did Britain reduce its empire?
(3) How and why did Britain become involved in the Cold War?
(4) Why did Britain's attitude to European cooperation and integration change?

How did the Second World War change the direction of British foreign policy?

Summary

Before the Second World War the aims of British foreign policy were to protect trade routes, defend the empire, help maintain a balance of power in Europe and generally provide security for the nation. Most senior politicians in government — regardless of party — adhered to this, although with the rise of Nazi Germany there had been some division over whether to take early direct action or to appease. **Neville Chamberlain**, prime minister of the National Government from 1937 to 1940, fully adhered to a policy of appeasement until the invasion of Poland by Hitler. The invasion is still considered by many historians to be the major cause of the war.

At the end of the war, in July 1945, a general election resulted in victory for the Labour Party led by **Clement Attlee**. With his foreign secretary, Ernest Bevin, he framed an approach to foreign affairs that seemed very similar to that of the interwar governments. The war had resulted in major changes in international affairs which Labour had to take into account. In particular, the USA had played a dominant role in resourcing the war and Russia had agreed to cooperate in a **Grand Alliance** to overcome the military might of Germany, Italy and Japan. You will need to know about how relations with the USA and Russia developed and how this affected the nature of British foreign policy.

Relations with the USA

Before the war the USA had adopted an isolationist approach to international affairs, preferring not to get directly involved in the business of other major nations. Once the war was under way and it was clear, after major German victories in central Europe, that Britain would be on its own, it became important for the British government to foster greater links with America. The American president, **F. D. Roosevelt**, was sympathetic to the British cause from the start and made available substantial resources through the passing of the **Lend-Lease Bill** of March 1941. Cooperation was strengthened with the publication of an Atlantic Charter in August 1941, which committed America to help defeat the evil of Nazi Germany. Despite this, it seemed that the USA was still reluctant to make a clear declaration of war.

A turning-point was the Japanese attack on the American naval fleet at Pearl Harbor in December 1941, which was followed immediately by Japan declaring war on the USA and Britain. America had no option but to show a total commitment to help win the war. From the beginning of 1942 to the end of the war there was a string of conferences between the Allied nations, which shaped the military strategy and determined what should happen to Germany after the war had finished. They also revealed much about the relative political, economic and military strengths of the Allies.

In January 1942 Roosevelt agreed to place 'Europe first' and announced that the United Nations (the Allied forces) would stick together to defeat Germany. This was strengthened by the inclusion of Russia, to form what was known as the Grand Alliance. From 1942 to 1944 Britain had to face a number of problems relating to the dynamics of the alliance.

First, as the USA quickly swamped parts of Europe with soldiers and armaments, Roosevelt demanded a significant say in military strategy. He pushed Britain to launch an invasion of France as quickly as possible but **Winston Churchill**, the British wartime leader, insisted on a more cautious approach and, using considerable skills of diplomacy, he encouraged Roosevelt to support first an invasion of Italy to weaken German resources.

Second, Roosevelt appeared to challenge Allied unity by paying more attention to the ideas of **Joseph Stalin**, the Russian leader, than to those of Churchill. This was especially true at the **Teheran Conference** in November 1943, which resulted in an agreement to invade France in May 1944 and Stalin promising to attack Japan after the German conflict. In return, Russia's claims over substantial parts of eastern Europe seemed to be accepted by Roosevelt, much to the annoyance of Churchill. This trend was reinforced at the **Yalta Conference** of February 1945, which had been set up to decide on the governance of Germany after its defeat, but also resulted in further concessions being made to Russia over the control of Poland.

Roosevelt died in April 1945 and was replaced by **Harry Truman**, and in the following month Germany surrendered. Churchill attempted to persuade Truman that Russia posed a serious threat to postwar peace and unity, but America was not convinced.

In addition, Truman, like Roosevelt, had some concerns about how British foreign policy would shape up in the postwar era and feared an over-reliance on strengthening the empire, which might damage American trade. Thus, by July 1945 relations with America had been slightly soured, but without American support the victory over Nazi Germany would not have been achieved. The war had emphasised to the British the economic, political and military strength of America and how significant its role was likely to be in the future in subduing the influence of Communist Russia.

Relations with Russia

During the interwar years British governments had been dominated by Conservative politicians who were fearful of Russia for ideological reasons. The Labour Party was obviously more sympathetic and large sections of the public did not support the idea of a Red threat. During the war Conservative opinion did not diminish and the left in Britain remained supportive, particularly after Russia managed to stave off defeat by Germany at the Battle of Stalingrad. Until 1941 the USSR had no time for Britain's wartime position, but Germany's **Operation Barbarossa**, the invasion of Russia, forced them to change. As with America, attempts to strengthen an alliance with Russia were made through the conference system. Churchill was always wary of Stalin's true intentions but even as late as February 1945, at Yalta, he declared his confidence in him. Atrocities committed by Polish Communists early in 1945 caused Churchill great anxiety, however. His communications with Truman mentioned an '**Iron Curtain**' that would be formed between Russian-controlled parts of Europe and land occupied by the Western Allies.

Russian actions during the war had been enough to convince Churchill that Russia would pose a major postwar threat. Attlee's government of 1945 was less sure of this, but it was a fear that was to influence British participation in the so-called **Cold War**.

The Potsdam Conference

The final conference of the Grand Alliance was held between 16 July and 2 August 1945 at Potsdam in Berlin. Progress was made in resolving issues over the short-term governance of Germany and reparations. There was disagreement on other policy areas, particularly on the future of Poland and other Eastern states. Tension was heightened when Truman informed Stalin that America had created an atomic bomb. The importance of the conference for Britain was that it was left unsure about its role in dealing with the long-term position of Germany and was worried about the spread of Russian influence in eastern Europe.

Conclusion

The direction of British foreign policy was forced to change during the war due to:
- the increasing influence of the USA in determining the direction of the war
- the perceived threat of the Soviet Union after the war

But foreign policy aims after the war were similar to those before, despite changes in government. Maintaining some kind of empire was considered crucial to the preservation of Britain's economic and political status.

How and why did Britain reduce its empire?

Summary

Britain reduced its empire through a process of decolonisation, giving independence to India and a range of countries in Africa and southeast Asia. Be aware that this started gradually but accelerated after 1959, marking a '**wind of change**'. You also need to be able to explain why decolonisation occurred, focusing particularly on economic factors and external influences.

Decolonisation

By 1964 most of the important colonies of the British empire had gained independence, including India (1947), Nigeria (1960) and Kenya (1963). This occurred in two stages. Before 1959 the British government had been occupied with resolving the issue of rising nationalism in India. This was complicated by divisions between Hindus, who controlled the majority of Indian provinces through the Indian National Congress, and Muslims, who campaigned for equal and fair representation through the Muslim League. The dilemma became difficult to resolve, but in August 1947 India and Pakistan were declared separate states to cater for the demands of each faction. British withdrawal followed almost immediately.

After 1947 Britain continued to have an interest in southeast Asia, mainly in Malaya. In 1948 the British government decided to group the different states and occupied areas of Malay into the Federation of Malaya. Malayan Chinese members of the federation feared that they would be dominated by Malaya and with the backing of Malayan Communists they organised a series of protests. These escalated into violent acts against British administrators, resulting in British troops being sent to Malaya to restore order. A guerrilla war ensued, continuing well into the 1950s, when some kind of order was restored. The Conservative government of the time believed it was absolutely necessary to make a stand against communism, but acknowledged that continued presence in the area would reap few benefits. Thus, in 1957 full independence was granted to Malaya.

Calls for independence among African states also gathered momentum after the Second World War, although only Ghana — previously known as the Gold Coast — achieved independence before 1959. In the mid-1950s in Kenya there had been considerable protest by members of the black population called the Mau Mau, who opposed plans for a union of African states. This would have involved joining Kenya, Uganda and Tanganyika to form the East African Federation and, as far as the Mau Mau were concerned, would have resulted in a loss of sovereignty and cultural identity.

The insurgence was suppressed by 1956 but it was clear that Britain would soon have to grant independence to Kenya and other black nations. Tanganyika was made independent in 1961, Uganda in 1962 and Kenya in 1962, although the Central Africa Federation (Nyasaland, Northern and Southern Rhodesia) continued to resist the 'wind of change' well after the 1960s.

The influence of the Suez Crisis

On 26 July 1956 the Egyptian leader, **Nasser**, announced that he was going to nationalise the Suez Canal Company, in which the British and French governments and entrepreneurs had major financial interests. There were numerous reasons for this, but the result was that Britain and France felt Nasser was abusing his authority and his actions were a challenge to world stability. The British and French oil trade was dependent on the Suez Canal and both countries had no option but to retaliate. **Anthony Eden**, the British prime minister, colluded with France and Israel to resolve the matter by force, without consulting the USA and other interested parties. Eden's approach proved to be something of a disaster and it took American intervention for the matter to be resolved finally in April 1957.

The Suez Crisis influenced Britain's colonial status as it:
- resulted in criticism from some Commonwealth countries over Britain's handling of the affair
- showed that the Commonwealth was not united enough to stand up to a potential dictator
- encouraged anti-colonial feelings and nationalism by making a hero out of Nasser
- generally reduced Britain's standing in the Middle East

content guidance

Reasons for a reduction in empire

Independence was granted to India, Pakistan, Ceylon and Burma in 1947–48 and control over Palestine abandoned in 1948, mainly due to internal pressures. Attlee's government did not see this as the beginning of the end of the empire. There was a hope that it would carry on in a different guise, namely a 'New' Commonwealth that would include the old 'white' dominions and the new independent states. This would continue to provide economic benefits to Britain and also act as a third major power in world politics, alongside the USA and USSR, and therefore balance out power.

The Conservative governments that followed Labour continued with the same approach, despite further claims for independence in Africa and disagreement among members of the New Commonwealth. In 1959, however, the prime minister, **Harold Macmillan**, appeared to change tack and made provision for a quick end to the empire, especially in Africa. In Cape Town, in 1960, he made his famous 'wind of change' speech, which acknowledged that the strength of national consciousness was so great in British-controlled African states that independence was inevitable and the granting of it was not to be delayed.

Historians are divided over why Macmillan's government changed policy. Reasons put forward include the following:
- **The rise of nationalism:** this is often stated as being the most important factor and certainly seemed to influence both France and Belgium, as well as Britain, in the dismantling of empires. It is evident, however, that not all citizens of empire states wanted independence and besides, if insurrection occurred, it would have been relatively easy for Britain to have used military force to quell it.
- **Military force:** suppression of uprisings was not a good option, as this may have resulted in widespread destruction and bloodshed, thereby diminishing Britain's world status. In addition, using troops to maintain law and order was increasingly costly and there was a possibility that national service would have to be reintroduced to bolster the armed forces as the number of disputes increased. This may have proved unacceptable to the general public.
- **The spread of communism:** Macmillan believed that devolving power to nationalists who supported the West would avert the spread of communism throughout Africa and other developing countries.
- **The economic burden:** in 1957 Macmillan commissioned an investigation into the cost of maintaining an empire, but the findings were inconclusive. Despite this, Macmillan was swayed towards rapid decolonisation when he realised that the loss of life, as in Malaya and Kenya, and financial burdens were likely to get worse. He matched this against the prospect of little further strategic gain and adopted a 'wind of change' philosophy.

Macmillan was well aware that political, economic and social conditions varied between and within the colonies, which meant that a blanket policy to decolonise was not possible. Nevertheless, his aim was to speed up the process so that the burdens of empire were lifted sooner rather than later.

Conclusion

Britain reduced its empire through a process of decolonisation that started gradually but speeded up after 1959. The main reasons for this were:

- the rise of nationalist movements in various parts of the empire
- the rising cost of maintaining an empire
- a belief that the nature of empire could be changed, resulting in the formation of a Commonwealth
- a realisation that it was increasingly difficult for Britain to maintain its position as a leading world power, as was illustrated by the Suez Crisis

Although these factors worked together, it was probably the cost of maintenance, coupled with the economic opportunities offered by devoting more time to cooperation with the rest of Europe, that led to the reduction of the empire.

How and why did Britain become involved in the Cold War?

Summary

The conflict that occurred between the USA and the USSR after the Second World War is referred to as the Cold War. It was characterised by tension, distrust and mutual hostility but no direct warfare. When studying this topic, make sure that you concentrate on why and how Britain became involved in the conflict. You will need to consider the attitudes of British politicians towards America and Russia and the relative importance of particular events such as the testing of atomic bombs, Marshall Aid, the creation of NATO and the Korean War.

Churchill and the Iron Curtain

During the Second World War Churchill, the British wartime leader, had been very wary of the intentions of Russia. There was uncertainty over whether Stalin was motivated by 'ambition or fear'. Churchill was concerned that Russian expansionism would eventually endanger European unity and, in particular, would severely disrupt British trade. By the end of the war Russia controlled most of eastern Europe and wanted to increase its sphere of influence in the Mediterranean.

In May 1945 Churchill had expressed his fears to the American president, Truman. He used the term 'Iron Curtain' to describe how Russia was appearing to partition off eastern Europe from the West. Churchill used the term again in March 1946 when making a famous speech at Fulton, Missouri. He tried to convince Americans that Russia posed the next threat to world peace and that it would exploit any sign of economic, political and military weakness shown by the West. The Labour government at home had hoped to strengthen relations with Russia but did not disagree with Churchill's views. The speech marked Britain's entry to the Cold War.

The development of the atom bomb

When atomic bombs were dropped on Hiroshima and Nagasaki in 1945 it was clear that the nature of warfare had changed dramatically. The possession of such awesome weapons would undoubtedly affect the power struggles between the nations. The bomb was initially developed as a collaborative project between Britain and the USA but by 1947 Britain had started to develop its own nuclear weaponry. Russia quickly followed suit and tested an atomic bomb in August 1949.

Britain continued to cooperate with America over the use of the bomb and by 1949 American B29 bombers carrying nuclear warheads were stationed on the British mainland. It was not clear who controlled the bombers until the early 1950s, however. Generally, the possession of the bomb and Britain's collaboration with America heightened the tensions during the early years of the Cold War.

Marshall Aid

The war drained Britain's economic resources and resulted in proposals to cut back on continental commitments after the war. One area targeted was Greece, where British forces had been sent to prevent a civil war and takeover by Communist rebels. By January 1947 Attlee decided to withdraw British troops. This prompted Truman to intervene and he encouraged Congress to provide financial aid for Greece and Turkey. This was known as the **Truman Doctrine** and marked a change in American foreign policy. Russia and communism were clearly seen as a threat to Europe, if not the world, and had to be restrained.

This was followed by an announcement in June 1947 by the American Secretary of State, Marshall, in which he offered economic aid to Europe. Marshall intended that money should be used by European nations to develop their own economic plans to restore prosperity, which would then close the door on communism. By April 1948, 16 western European nations had responded by forming the **Organisation for European Economic Cooperation** (OEEC), which would work to a 4-year plan to reconstruct faltering European economies. By 1951 the OEEC had received nearly $12 billion from the USA, with Britain taking $2.6 billion — by far the biggest chunk.

The implications for Britain were significant. First, Marshall Aid would help combat economic problems created by a substantial balance of payments deficit and would take the place of wartime loans, which had run out. Second, the rift between Russia and the West widened further. Stalin wanted nothing to do with Marshall Aid and condemned it as 'dollar imperialism'. He blamed America for creating further disunity by attempting to gain economic control over western Europe while isolating the East.

The creation of NATO

The North Atlantic Treaty Organisation was formed in January 1950 by America, Britain and ten other countries. The aim of the organisation was to protect individual members against military action by promising a collective response against aggressors. Although there was some uncertainty over how strong the organisation would prove to be, it was another example of America's commitment to offer protection to western Europe. From the beginning Britain made available its armed forces and the needs of NATO allies were considered when foreign policy decisions were made.

The Korean War

In June 1950 Communist North Korea invaded the South. Many Americans and British believed this was instigated by Stalin in an attempt to divert American support away from western Europe, leaving it vulnerable to Russian pressure. Both America and Britain reacted quickly and, under the flag of the United Nations, troops were sent to defend South Korea. Despite the intervention of China, United Nations troops eventually managed to push back the invading forces and hold a defensive line on the 38th parallel, the border between North and South Korea. American and British politicians decided to hold this position despite calls to enter the North and defeat the Communists once and for all. MacArthur, the military leader of the UN, even called for an invasion of China, but was sacked by Truman to prevent the possibility of the conflict escalating. Nevertheless, the war dragged on until 1953, with considerable British and American casualties.

The war was significant for Britain for two reasons. First, America showed an even greater level of support for NATO through the provision of military hardware. Second, it strengthened the so-called '**special relationship**' with America, a concept fashioned by Churchill during the Second World War and developed further after 1951.

Conclusion

Britain became involved in the Cold War due to:
- fear over the spread of communism, epitomised by Churchill's Iron Curtain speeches
- a perceived need to participate in the arms race and the production of nuclear weapons
- the view that American financial and military support was necessary to avert a third world war
- a commitment made to western European defence through the setting up of NATO

Why did Britain's attitude to European cooperation and integration change?

Summary

By 1945 Britain's attitude towards European cooperation and integration was one of caution. British politicians were generally not averse to working closely with other European countries to reconstruct economies and strengthen military capabilities for defence purposes. At the same time this had to be balanced against a lack of economic resources, a commitment to maintaining a semblance of an empire, and calls from large sections of the public to retain national sovereignty. Initially, Britain took a rather negative view of forming institutions that fully integrated Europe, but by the early 1960s senior politicians had changed tack. You will need to be able to explain why this was the case, taking careful note of the influences on British attitudes and how they changed up to 1963.

Attitudes in Britain to the continent

These can be discussed with respect to military and economic cooperation, the importance of empire, and American and European interests.

- **Military cooperation:** there were mixed views over this, but with America's support for the rearmament of Germany the British showed interest in a unified approach to the defence of Europe. This was demonstrated through discussion about the **Pleven Plan** of October 1950 and proposals for a **European Defence Community** (EDC). The EDC project collapsed in August 1954 when the French National Assembly withdrew support. NATO became the institution for providing a level of military integration and a vehicle for the monitoring of German rearmament after Germany was admitted in 1955.

- **Economic cooperation:** this proved more problematic, although a positive step was taken in 1948 with the formation of the OEEC. There was general concern up to the early 1960s that an integrated approach to economic affairs would lead to a lack of control over British economic institutions, and damage to agriculture and industry.

- **Empire:** Britain acknowledged that it would have to relinquish its grip over parts of the empire. Some kind of empire was considered necessary, however, as it provided both raw materials for industry and a ready market for British goods. At the end of the war there were about four times as many people living in the empire than in western Europe but, as was proved by the 1960s, with considerably less purchasing power.

- **America:** Churchill believed that there was a 'special relationship' with America, although he also recognised that in many ways America was in the driving seat when it came to international economic and political affairs. Britain had to balance the need to cooperate with America with a wish to hold a prominent position in the affairs of Europe.

- **Europe:** Britain felt that a degree of cooperation and participation in European military and economic projects was necessary to maintain stability, especially in view of the threat from Communist Russia and uncertainty over the future of Germany. But issues of resourcing and sovereignty consistently prevented total commitment until the early 1960s.

Opposition to the Schuman Plan

In May 1950 the French foreign minister, **Robert Schuman**, announced a plan for a **European Coal and Steel Community** (ECSC). This would allow the free movement of coal and steel throughout member countries. Britain opposed the plan for two reasons. First, it would have to sacrifice an element of national sovereignty, as the ECSC would be controlled by a supranational organisation. Second, it was feared that the British coal and steel industries would suffer and there would be damage to Labour's nationalisation of industry programme.

In April 1951 the ECSC was put into operation, consisting of France, West Germany, Italy, Belgium, Luxembourg and the Netherlands. It was such a success that a special conference was held at Messina in 1955 to consider how the concept could be developed, but Britain remained aloof and detached.

Opposition to the Treaty of Rome

The success of the ECSC prompted member states to develop a bigger version of a united European economic community. In March 1957 the Treaty of Rome was signed, which established the **European Economic Community** (known also as the **Common Market**). This aimed to protect member states from 'external' competition, allow labour and capital to move freely within the market and remove 'internal' restrictions on trade. Supranational institutions were established to run the EEC. They consisted of the **Council of Ministers**, the **European Commission**, the **European Assembly** and the **Court of Justice**.

Harold Macmillan's Conservative government declined to take part. This was the second occasion on which Britain was said to have 'missed the bus'. A main objection was based on the need to abide by the decisions of supranational bodies, which, it was feared, would lead to a loss of national sovereignty. Another argument was that trade with the empire (which was a bigger market) would be damaged and that British agriculture would be treated less favourably than its continental counterparts.

Macmillan's U-turn

Although there was initially strong opposition in Britain to joining the EEC, within 2 years Macmillan had made an application for membership. It was soon realised that Britain might be excluded from trading with the EEC and that this European market was potentially more lucrative than that of the empire. In 1960 Britain had attempted to compensate for non-inclusion by forming the **European Free Trade Area** with other western European nations in a similar position. Many politicians saw this as a 'poor man's' version of the EEC, and by October 1961 Macmillan had won support for his U-turn from his cabinet (after a reshuffle), Parliament, the Conservative Party and the general public.

Unfortunately for Macmillan, **Adenauer** (the German chancellor) and **de Gaulle** (the French prime minister) colluded to ensure that Britain's application for membership was rejected and that there was a veto on further negotiations. This seemed to be due to a general distrust of Britain's links with America and the Commonwealth. On 14 January 1963 de Gaulle formally announced his objections. Macmillan was bitterly disappointed, although there was a more mixed reaction from colleagues and the general public who were less certain about the potential benefits of joining.

Conclusion

Britain's attitude to European cooperation and integration changed due to:
- the success of the ECSC and the formation of the EEC
- the relative decline in the importance of empire and Commonwealth markets
- the purchasing power of western Europeans and the relative growth in importance of western European markets
- a level of caution about the 'special relationship' with America
- a realisation of the way in which the EEC seemed to strengthen the positions of France and West Germany within Europe

One factor is not necessarily more important than any other, although concerns over trade relationships and economic growth seem to have been paramount.

Postwar Britain, 1945–64

The four key issues for study and examination are:
(1) How profound were the changes introduced by the Labour government, 1945–51?
(2) Why did the Labour Party win the election of 1945 so overwhelmingly, yet lose in 1951?
(3) Why did the Conservatives remain in power from 1951 to 1964?
(4) Why did the Labour Party win the election of 1964?

How profound were the changes introduced by the Labour government, 1945–51?

Summary

The changes introduced by the Labour governments of 1945–51 were characterised by social reforms in housing, health, education and National Insurance. The governments also pushed ahead with the nationalisation of key industries. You need to know about these changes in some depth and be able to assess how revolutionary they were. You also need to be aware of how they impacted upon British society.

The expectations of the electorate in 1945

Once the war against Nazi Germany had been won, it was clear that the British population in general looked forward to a new, reconstructed society that would be a break from the past. There seemed to be a common desire not to return to the bad old days of the interwar years, characterised by high unemployment and poverty.

A greater awareness of social issues among all classes had arisen during the war, mainly as a result of shared adversity. In particular, the communal air-raid shelters of the Blitz, evacuation and rationing all led to increased understanding of the difficulties faced by many people in the poorest parts of Britain. There seemed to be a willingness to adopt a more cooperative approach to solving social problems and an acceptance that governments had to intervene on a wider scale for the benefit of the whole of society.

The social reforms of the Labour governments of 1945–51

Although Winston Churchill, the Conservative Party leader, had proved to be a great wartime leader, he had not been very enthusiastic about plans for postwar reform. He made it clear during the war that he thought it was important to focus on achieving military victory and not to make promises about postwar improvements that might not be achievable.

The Labour Party took the opposite view and encouraged thinking and planning about how the living standards of the population could be improved. Their ideas were based partly on investigation carried out during the interwar years, but also on the work of the civil servant **William Beveridge**. Beveridge had been asked by the wartime National Government to investigate the workings of the national insurance scheme, but he used this as an opportunity to offer a blueprint to tackle what he called the 'five giants' in society: want, idleness, squalor, disease and ignorance. In 1942 he published a report which outlined how this could be achieved. Beveridge showed how the 'giants' were interlinked and argued that only a comprehensive and universal approach to tackling social ills, based on a national insurance scheme, would work.

Beveridge's proposals were extremely popular with the public, and the Labour Party realised the political significance of using the report as the basis for reform. Churchill, however, was critical, and when Labour announced its plans to create a welfare state for everyone he became insulting, claiming that Labour was about to introduce a Gestapo-like approach to governing. In other words, the party would have total control over the lives of British citizens. This simply strengthened Labour's resolve and turned voters against Churchill. In 1945 Labour achieved a historic victory in the general election. The new government immediately set about implementing its plan for social and economic reform:

- **Housing:** from 1945 to 1951 just over 1 million houses were built and about half a million temporary homes ('prefabs') were provided. Most of these were for working-class people to rent. Given the economic problems faced at the end of the war, which affected the availability of building resources, Labour's achievement in this area was very impressive.
- **Health:** a **National Health Service** was created under the guidance of **Aneurin Bevan** and came into operation from July 1948. It provided free health care for all. This was undoubtedly a radical policy, although schemes for such a service had already been drawn up in the interwar period. It was a particular triumph for Bevan, who used considerable skill to overcome opposition from the **British**

content guidance

Medical Association over the issue of the employment of salaried doctors by the government.

- **Education:** Labour invested quite heavily in the system laid out in the **1944 Education Act**. This created a tripartite system of secondary education, which was made free to all. Some critics claimed that this went against Labour philosophy and thought there should have been a move towards a comprehensive secondary schooling system. But many Labour politicians believed that it would encourage clever working-class children to thrive, particularly if 'parity of esteem' was maintained between all three types of secondary school (grammar, technical and secondary modern). This is considered by a number of historians to be the most conservative policy adopted by Labour.

- **National Insurance:** a universal national insurance scheme was introduced in 1946. It was backed up by the **National Assistance Act** of 1948, which provided a safety net for those not covered by National Insurance. There were also measures to provide state support for workers suffering from industrial injuries. Underpinning this was Labour's economic policy to achieve and maintain full employment, which was based on the ideas of Beveridge and the economist John Maynard Keynes. The concept of insurance was not new but the idea of covering everyone in society was. In principle, it was a very sound scheme to tackle poverty but, as subsequent governments soon realised, it was weakened by rising levels of inflation.

- **Nationalisation:** nationalisation of major industries had been a major part of Labour's policy since the end of the First World War. In 1945 it was claimed it would lead to greater efficiency. The state would set up public corporations to run strategic industries for the benefit of all. The **Bank of England** (1946) was the first to be nationalised and this was followed by civil aviation (1946), coal, cable and wireless (1947) and inland transport, electricity and gas (1948). The nationalisation of iron and steel was more controversial as it involved manufacturing industry, but it was eventually pushed through in 1951. Workers in nationalised industries seemed to benefit, as generally the programme was very much in line with the idea of the '**Socialist Commonwealth**' that the party had promised in its 1945 election manifesto. Nevertheless, maintaining the industries became problematic and costly and was certainly not part of a move towards a planned economy.

Taken as a whole, the social reforms of the Labour governments before 1951 were probably the best that could be provided, given the circumstances. When broken down into areas, however, some reforms were clearly more radical than others and most were built on ideas that had emerged before the war.

Conclusion

The changes introduced by Labour governments 1945–51 were profound in so far as:
- they aimed to be universal and comprehensive
- they looked to create a new society rather than re-establish an old one
- they constituted an optimum form of provision to create a 'welfare state'

However:

- many of Labour's ideas were not new
- some policies were rather cautious, such as those relating to housing and education
- some would argue that 'optimum provision' was an exaggeration and that there was still a lot more that Labour could have done

Why did the Labour Party win the election of 1945 so overwhelmingly, yet lose in 1951?

Summary

To answer this question you need to understand why voters turned against the great wartime leader and hero, Winston Churchill, to vote for Clement Attlee and the Labour Party. Although Churchill was adored by many, the Conservative Party in general was associated with the economic and social problems of the interwar years. Labour, on the other hand, was seen as the reforming party, which would bring a more prosperous future.

By 1951 the Labour Party was struggling to maintain power. It was a divided party that was having a hard time dealing with problems relating to wages, rationing, the balance of payments and government expenditure. The Conservatives, on the other hand, had gathered momentum and reorganised. They were ready for another term of office.

The Labour victory in 1945

The European campaign in the Second World War effectively ended when, on 7 May 1945, Germany made an unconditional surrender. British politicians decided that the wartime coalition government should be ended sooner rather than later and a general election was called for July 1945. It proved to be a landslide victory for the Labour Party. Labour won 393 seats, the Conservatives 213 and the Liberals 12. For many this was an outstanding victory, particularly as Churchill, the Conservative leader, had been a great wartime hero. The reasons for this result are manifold.

First, in Labour's manifesto — 'Let Us Face the Future' — they promised far greater state intervention to improve the lot of everyone in society. A more collectivist approach certainly seemed acceptable as a result of the shared adversity that stemmed from the war through rationing, the Blitz, evacuation and conscription. In particular, the middle classes appeared to show more acceptance that something rather drastic had to be done to help the poorest members of society. Thus, there was the beginning of a marked change in attitude towards the wish for a fairer and more equal society, which accorded with what Labour stood for.

Second, there was no great rival to Labour to challenge the Conservatives. The Liberals' fortunes had dwindled dramatically and the other socialist parties were insignificant.

Third, Labour already had some experience of government and Labour politicians had performed well during the war. The party generated an air of confidence and dynamism that appealed to the electorate.

Finally, the Conservatives' manifesto virtually ignored the idea of social reform as outlined in the Beveridge Report and focused more on international affairs. Churchill likened Labour's policies to totalitarianism and Nazi-like control by the state. Some historians highlight Churchill's attack as unnecessary but crucial in alienating the public. In reality, the 'people' probably took little notice. They were more interested in practical issues relating to working and living conditions and voted for the party that had most to offer. That was Labour.

Government problems to 1951

Labour remained in power until 1951. In the September general election of that year the Conservatives gained 321 seats, Labour 295 and the Liberals 6. Of significance was the fact that many important gains by the Conservatives were made in middle-class areas in London and the southeast more generally.

During Labour's 6 years in office it introduced the welfare state, integral to which was the control of high and persistent unemployment, which had been the major domestic problem of the interwar period. The nationalisation of key industries was also pushed ahead, although there were more mixed feelings about this. On the whole, Labour's achievement was remarkable given the conditions of the time, and yet it survived in office for only 6 years.

From 1945 to 1947 Labour seemed to be in total control of the economy, but the winter of 1947 was a turning-point in its fortunes. A fuel crisis damaged industrial production, unemployment rose and trade was adversely affected. There was also concern that inflation might increase. As a result, certain measures were carried out which were unpopular:

- **Rationing:** this wartime phenomenon continued until 1949 for clothes and 1950 for some basic foods (not including bread) and petrol. It was considered necessary because of import controls, but was hated, especially as it meant the continuation of a 'black market'.
- **Wage freezes:** a policy of wage restraint was adopted in March 1948 and lasted until 1950. Although designed to combat inflation, it was also significant as it was balanced by the introduction of a wealth tax, which upset the middle classes.
- **The balance of payments problem:** probably the biggest problem for Attlee in his first term of office was how to improve Britain's international trading position. The winter crisis of 1947 reduced exports but imports continued to rise, especially from America. The latter were not cheap and a drain on foreign currency, particularly the dollar, soon occurred. Ironically, the situation was eased by using

money from a loan provided by America, but this was not a long-term solution. Import controls were also tried, which affected decisions about rationing. There was no major improvement until **Sir Stafford Cripps** took over from Dalton as chancellor of the exchequer in November 1947. Through a relaxation of industrial controls and new incentives for industry, exports increased, and by early 1948 there was a balance of payments surplus. This trend was reversed again in 1949, but was checked by a devaluation of the pound. By 1951 exports were about three times above the level existing at the beginning of the Second World War.

Although there was obvious success in dealing with the balance of payments problems, there were knock-on effects. A rift emerged over what policy to adopt, with Attlee receiving much criticism. Furthermore, Cripps used wage freezes and continued rationing to stabilise the economy, which was unpopular, and when he felt the ship was steady, he pushed to make cuts in public expenditure, which caused further disagreement. All of this did not bode well for future success in general elections.

Cripps got his own way and expenditure cuts were made, but Labour still managed to win the February 1950 general election. There were signs, though, that the middle classes were getting restless over Labour's austerity programme. Although the economy was buoyant by the early 1950s, Labour's commitment to the Korean War from January 1951 onwards meant increased expenditure on armaments and an extension of the conscription programme. Pressure was placed on **Hugh Gaitskell**, now chancellor, to make cuts in expenditure elsewhere. This included the Health Service, a move that was bitterly opposed by left-wingers in the party. Thus, once again, division over economic policy threatened to damage Labour's prospects of staying in power.

Internal divisions

Divisions within the postwar Labour Party first emerged in 1947 when Cripps attempted to gain support to oust Attlee and replace him with Bevin. Attlee was viewed as inept, but Cripps backed off from challenging him once he was given the post of chancellor of the exchequer. As Cripps manufactured what is commonly referred to as an '**age of austerity**', further divisions emerged. The prospect of wide-ranging cuts in expenditure angered the left wing of the party, especially Aneurin Bevan. As the man who introduced the NHS, Bevan was deeply hurt and insulted when Gaitskell, in his April 1951 budget, brought in charges for dentures and spectacles. He refused to accept that necessary funds could not be made by cutting the rearmament programme and therefore decided to resign from the government. He was followed by **Harold Wilson** and John Freeman. Attlee had seemingly failed to reconcile differences in the party and, partly due also to a re-emerging balance of payments crisis, he decided to call a general election in October 1951.

Conservative reorganisation

While Labour was in power the Conservative Party, driven by the reformers **Butler** and **Woolton**, attempted to reorganise and modernise. This was done in the following ways:

- A campaign was launched by Woolton to bolster grassroots support and raise party funds. The money would be used to revamp both Central Office and regional associations.
- **Maxwell-Fyfe** introduced a plan to restrict contributions made by individuals, which had previously influenced their possible selection as parliamentary candidates. This was seen as making the party more democratic, but was in fact rather cosmetic.
- In 1947 Butler published the **Industrial Charter**, which showed commitment by the Conservatives to a welfare state and a greater degree of collectivism. It also attempted to show how socialist-type ideas were not incompatible with the concept of individualism and the free market.

The reorganisation of the Conservatives certainly had a role to play in enabling them to gain victory in 1951. But the margin of their win was small and many historians argue that the result was due more to the electorate's disillusionment with Labour than a newly found admiration for the Conservatives. It should also be noted that the Conservatives were helped by the Liberals' decision to field only a small number of candidates. It is likely that old Liberal supporters were now more inclined to vote Tory than Labour.

Conclusion

The main reason for Labour's dramatic victory in 1945 was that it promised something of a revolution in social reform, whereas Churchill and the Conservatives adopted a more precautionary approach. The decline of Labour by 1951 was due to a range of interrelated factors. Labour was faced with many economic problems, which, with hindsight, it tackled effectively. But there were internal divisions over the long-term direction that Labour should take and, ironically, over the very economic measures that proved so successful. The electorate, particularly the middle classes, were also frustrated by the economic measures taken, which appeared to hit them more than any other group. The reorganisation of the Conservative Party reinforced the prospects of a Tory victory that was almost inevitable.

Why did the Conservatives remain in power from 1951 to 1964?

Summary

Although the Conservatives remained in power from 1951 to 1964, the various governments were not without problems. You should be aware of the differences and similarities between the Conservative governments of the period. You will also need to know about the strengths and successes of the Conservatives, but this should be balanced against the problems faced by other parties, especially Labour.

Social changes and the comparative prosperity of the 1950s

Both the Churchill (1951–55) and Eden (1955–57) governments were able to build on the successes of Attlee's postwar Labour government and tackle the problems that had been left, particularly those relating to the economy. Butler, the chancellor of the exchequer under Churchill, showed considerable ability in turning a balance of payments deficit into a significant surplus by 1952. He also reduced income tax and abolished food rationing, and generally this heralded an overall rise in living standards. This was characterised by an increase in the purchase of a range of consumer goods such as cars, television sets, refrigerators and washing machines. There was also a rise in home ownership. Nevertheless, there was an element of luck about this. The Korean War came to an end in 1953, resulting in a reduced drain on government finances, and there was a 'natural' fall in import prices.

Churchill's government also made strides in social policy. Social services were expanded and a substantial increase in house building occurred. This seemed to be greatly welcomed by the public; so much so that even when a more negative step was taken — to introduce prescription charges — there was little outcry.

There was a slight blip for the Conservatives during Eden's government. Although it is fair to say that there was further consolidation of the welfare state, Eden struggled to deal with economic affairs successfully. There were signs that inflation might get out of hand and have a detrimental impact on living standards. Eden's strengths were supposedly in foreign affairs, but he failed to deal effectively with a crisis over the governance of the Suez Canal and this lost him his party's support. In January 1957 he resigned and was replaced by Macmillan.

Macmillan as prime minister

In many ways Macmillan was like Churchill. He was fairly moderate, wanting to adopt a 'middle way' in politics and, when necessary, was cautious and pragmatic. But he was slightly younger than Churchill and was entering his first term as prime minister. He wanted to show that he could be dynamic, focused and highly professional in his post. Although he was keen to 'get things done', he was also a thinker and planner. Macmillan's cabinet consisted of many like-minded people, all of whom were aiming to maintain levels of prosperity achieved by earlier governments. Macmillan's personal qualities undoubtedly helped the Conservatives achieve a major election victory in 1959 and it seemed rather apt that he was dubbed '**Supermac**' by the media.

Despite the continued threat of rising inflation, Macmillan insisted that there should be no expenditure cuts, as he thought these would result in unemployment, a greater evil. His chancellor of the exchequer, Heathcoat-Amory, introduced more tax cuts, which again pleased the public. By the middle of 1960, however, the economy had started to spiral out of control, with rampant inflation and the worst balance of payments deficit since 1951.

In March 1963 a scandal broke out concerning the relationship between the minister of war, John Profumo, and Christine Keeler, a prostitute. The Conservative Party entered a period of increasing unpopularity, and in 1963 Macmillan resigned as prime minister.

Labour problems, 1951–64

There were three main problems for the Labour Party during this period:

- **Bevanites:** the Bevanites were followers of Aneurin ('Nye') Bevan, a staunch socialist and critic of the Labour 'old guard'. Until 1955 Bevan and his supporters consistently criticised and opposed the policies of the Labour leader, Attlee. A major rift occurred in the party, which pivoted on the direction that Labour should take. The Bevanites wanted adherence to a socialist programme and Clause Four of the party constitution (see p. 30). Opponents wanted the party to take a more moderate approach.
- **Gaitskell:** in May 1955 Hugh Gaitskell took over from Attlee as party leader and surprisingly gained the support of Bevan. Gaitskell still struggled to establish party unity, however, particularly over the issues of nationalisation and defence policy. There was much debate over whether the Labour Party should support the idea of Britain maintaining a nuclear deterrent, and pontificating over this led to some supporters drifting away to join the **Campaign for Nuclear Disarmament** (CND).
- **The 1959 election:** Labour was soundly beaten at this election, and much of the blame was placed on the party's image. It was argued that Labour was 'old-fashioned' and was not in tune with the new consumer-based society emerging in Britain. It was also associated with trade unionism, industrial unrest, working-class politics and a restricted view of how the country should be run. Gaitskell had some success in encouraging younger Labour members to draft a revisionist plan, and by the early 1960s he had restored some unity to the party.

At the annual party conference in October 1961 Gaitskell managed to gain endorsement for a policy to support NATO and the possession of nuclear weapons. The following year he strengthened his position further by opposing entry into the European Common Market, a stance that appeared to be supported by most of the population. Just as the party seemed to be gathering momentum, Gaitskell died unexpectedly in January 1963. He was succeeded by Harold Wilson.

Conclusion

The Conservative Party remained in power from 1951 to 1964 as a result of:

- the skill of certain politicians, particularly Churchill and Macmillan
- appropriate economic policies
- fortuitous circumstances, such as favourable international trading conditions
- splits in the Labour Party
- the out-of-date image and policies of the Labour Party

It is hard to say what the most important factors were, although on balance the Conservatives were certainly more unified than Labour and had politicians who were able to maintain noticeable improvements in living standards.

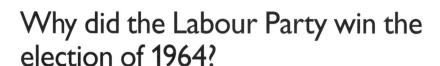

Why did the Labour Party win the election of 1964?

Summary

The Labour Party won a narrow victory in the 1964 election, due partly to economic problems that Conservative chancellors had struggled to deal with since 1960. The Conservatives were also plagued by scandal and a leadership crisis, which dented their credibility. Labour, on the other hand, began to surge forward under the more dynamic 'modern' leadership of Harold Wilson, who proved more than a match for Macmillan. Your main task is to judge what the most significant factors were in determining the end of 13 years of Conservative dominance.

The declining fortunes of the Conservative Party

In 1960 the Conservatives faced a huge balance of payments deficit and wage inflation. By the end of the year the chancellor of the exchequer, **Selwyn Lloyd**, had set up the **National Economic Development Council** ('Neddy') and the **National Incomes Commission** ('Nicky') in an attempt to deal with the problems. This was followed in July 1961 with a '**pay purse**' policy, which attempted to limit pay increases to public sector workers. Due to opposition from the TUC and public sector unions, Lloyd's deflationary policies were a failure. In addition, they were linked to an increase in unemployment and by July 1962 Lloyd was considered to be so inept that he was replaced by **Reginald Maudling**. Despite attempts to reflate the economy, Maudling fared no better, and by October 1964 there was a government deficit of £750 million.

Conservative supporters reacted by turning to the Liberal Party, which started to make considerable ground in by-elections. Macmillan believed a quick change of image for the government was needed and in July 1962 he sacked a third of his cabinet, replacing them with younger members. This was seen as an overreaction by many staunch party members and caused a rift.

Macmillan also faced criticism for his handling of the Kim Philby spy scandal of March 1963 and the **Profumo Affair** of June 1963. The latter in particular caused a stir as Macmillan gave full backing to Profumo, who denied allegations about involvement with a prostitute, Christine Keeler. As Keeler was also involved with a Soviet military official, this was obviously a serious business. Profumo eventually admitted he had lied and Macmillan was made to look foolish.

In October 1963 Macmillan fell ill, prompting him to offer his resignation as prime minister. This led to a leadership crisis, with Maudling, Lord Hailsham and Rab Butler being put forward as possible successors. Macmillan expressed his concern about all three, particularly Butler, and pushed for the appointment of the largely unknown Lord Home. Macmillan thought that Maudling was too young, Hailsham rather selfish and Butler weak. Home was solid, dependable, calm and collected. To the surprise and consternation of many, he was given the job. He quickly renounced his peerage, entering the House of Commons in November 1963 as **Sir Alec Douglas-Home**.

The impact of Wilson as Labour leader

Harold Wilson replaced Hugh Gaitskell as Labour leader in January 1963. Wilson had the reputation of being an idealist and a supporter of left-wing policies. By early 1963, though, he seemed to have changed, adopting a more practical outlook; he wanted to portray Labour as a modern party. He made a number of dynamic speeches on the theme of 'modernisation' in the years immediately following his appointment. Wilson believed that Britain would only continue to flourish under a new wave of scientific and technological change, and referred to the '**white heat of the technological revolution**'. This fresh, exciting approach to Labour policy seemed to reunite the party and to give it more impetus.

The 1964 election

Douglas-Home called a general election for 15 October 1964. The Conservatives campaigned on a theme of continued prosperity, arguing that theirs was the only party that could maintain steady improvements in living standards. Wilson, however, attacked them for being complacent, claiming that there had been '13 wasted years' under their rule. The concept of modernisation was forcefully expressed in the Labour Party manifesto entitled 'The New Britain', and it obviously appealed to the electorate. Wilson argued that his approach would lead to continuous and accelerating economic growth, which the Conservatives had failed to achieve.

The final result left Labour with 317 seats and the Conservatives with 304 seats. The Conservative vote had fallen by well over a million from 1959 and that of Labour stayed roughly the same. Labour did especially well in London and the southeast, whereas the bulk of Conservative support was from the north, the Midlands, Scotland and Wales.

Conclusion

The Labour Party won the 1964 election due to:
- the Conservatives' mishandling of economic problems from 1960 onwards
- the declining popularity of Macmillan
- the ineffectiveness of Douglas-Home
- the appeal of Wilson and the 'white heat of the technological revolution'

Questions
&
Answers

This section of the book advises you on how to answer the type of essay question used to assess this module. Sample answers are provided for each question, showing band-I and band-III responses.

Examiner comments (preceded by the icon *e*) are given for each of the answers. They point out strengths and weaknesses, and indicate possible ways in which the answers could be improved.

Examination questions

The examination paper will have a choice of eight questions, two on each study topic. You will be asked to answer one question from the two on your chosen study topic in 45 minutes. You will be given a mark out of 45 which is then doubled. The doubling occurs simply for statistical reasons so that a final AS History mark out of 300 can be awarded. Thus, the allocation of marks for the three AS units is as follows:

- document study — maximum mark = 120
- English history period study — maximum mark = 45 × 2 = 90
- European and American history period study — maximum mark = 45 × 2 = 90

This gives a final total of 120 + 90 + 90 = 300.

Your essay is marked using both general (generic) and question-specific mark schemes. The general mark scheme sets out the *general* areas of knowledge, understanding and skill that you are expected display, e.g. an ability to evaluate key issues convincingly and relevantly. The question-specific mark scheme indicates *specific* areas of content that your answers could display, e.g. a question on the 1926 General Strike might demand details about long, medium and short-term causes.

Examiners are asked to stick mainly to the generic mark scheme and only use the question-specific mark scheme to check on details and arguments that could be included in successful answers.

The essay question will require you to focus on evaluation. This means showing an ability to apply historical skills relevant to the question. In particular, you are likely to be asked to:

- analyse, i.e. take a historical issue apart and identify the relative importance of each part
- assess, i.e. weigh up the importance of a particular issue or issues
- compare, i.e. look for similarities and differences between historical issues; often used in conjunction with cause and consequence
- explain, i.e. say why a historical event occurred

Types of question

Questions can broadly be split into two types:

(1) Explanatory questions:
- Why did...?
- Why was...?
- Explain why...

(2) Discursive questions:
- How far did...?
- To what extent do you agree that...?
- Assess the view that...

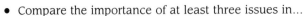

- Compare the importance of at least three issues in...
- How effectively did...?
- How valid is the claim that...?
- '(a quotation)' How far do you agree with this point of view?
- How accurate is the view that...?

For a high-quality answer to any type of question, it is essential to frame your arguments. **Explanatory questions** require a set of reasons for a historical event or action to be presented within an analytical structure. It is usually best to start discussing the most important reasons, making a justification for your choice in the conclusion. **Discursive questions** demand balanced assessment of different arguments. Whatever the type of question, you will be expected to show a wide range of in-depth knowledge and understanding of the issue being looked at.

Band-I answers are full and accurate and display a high level of understanding. Band-III answers are more descriptive and may drift towards narrative. A more detailed version of descriptors for these bands is given below.

Band I (36–45 out of 45 marks)

The response evaluates the key issues and deals with the perspective(s) in the question convincingly and relevantly. The answer is successful in showing a high level of understanding. It focuses on explanation rather than description or narrative. The quality of historical knowledge supporting the argument is sound and is communicated in a clear and effective manner. The answer is well organised. The writing shows accuracy in grammar, punctuation and spelling.

At the higher level (40–45), responses effectively justify why one factor is the most important and will also explain why other factors are less important. The answer demonstrates a sense of judgement by discriminating between the different types of factors. How factors are linked to each other is addressed.

At the lower level (36–39), responses justify why one factor is most important, but the explanation of why others are less so is less effective. There is some attempt to classify and draw links between factors.

Band III (27–31 out of 45 marks)

The response is reasonably successful in evaluating key issues and in dealing with perspective(s) in the question convincingly and relevantly.

It is reasonably successful in showing a good level of understanding. The answer tends to be descriptive or narrative in approach, but the argument depends on some analysis. The quality of recall, selection and accuracy of historical knowledge, applied relevantly, is mostly sound and is communicated in a clear and effective manner. The organisation is uneven but there is a sustained argument.

The quality of historical knowledge supporting the argument is satisfactory and is communicated in a competent manner. The comments miss some points or are less satisfactory in terms of supporting historical knowledge. The response recognises the need to deal with a number of factors and may well provide some very limited argument as to why one factor is more important than others. A list of factors is dealt with and explained effectively but the explanation of the most important ones, or of linkages, is slight and undeveloped. The writing generally shows accuracy in grammar, punctuation and spelling.

Notice how the descriptors are fairly similar, but also how there is a difference within band I. The gap between bands I and III can be bridged by focusing more on explanation and analysis, ensuring that balanced judgements and conclusions are drawn. This does not mean to say that band-III answers contain no analysis, but only that there is more of a tendency to drift towards description.

Liberals and Labour, 1899–1918

To what extent did the Liberal social reforms from 1906 to 1914 lay the foundation for a modern welfare state?

■ ■ ■

Band-I answer to question 1

Welfare state implies the optimum or best possible welfare provision for the whole of the population that could be made at a given point in time by a government. From the time of the landslide election victory of 1906 to the beginning of the First World War the Liberal government implemented a number of reforms that aimed to improve conditions for children, the elderly, the sick and the unemployed. But it is debatable as to whether its policies laid the foundation for a welfare state, as they did not constitute an integrated package of measures that covered all members of the particular groups. Maybe it is best to see the reforms as a limited response to a mix of economic, political and social pressures, which would enable a particular party to stay in power.

> *e* This answer starts well. A definition of 'modern welfare state' is offered and a plan of how the question is going to be tackled is then outlined. It is clear that the candidate aims to frame an argument and stick closely to the instruction in the question, i.e. 'To what extent…'. Such a clear, balanced introduction is particularly impressive as there is no OCR assessment requirement that states essays should have a clearly defined start. Obviously, though, without a good introduction an answer is likely to lack organisation and will have less chance of reaching the higher grades.

When the Liberals entered government in 1906 they did so without a detailed plan for social reform. In fact, their victory is often attributed to the failures of the Conservatives rather than their own strengths and promises made to the general public. It has been pointed out that a number of the members of the cabinet were 'new Liberals', i.e. politicians who were willing to move away from the traditional *laissez-faire* and free trade-based type of liberalism to one that promoted more government intervention and protectionism. The 'new Liberals' seemed to be more tuned in to the significance of various economic, political and social changes. This included economic competition from Germany and the USA, the rise of the Labour Party and the influence of socialism, and revelations by Booth and Rowntree about rising levels of poverty. This suggests that from the beginning there may have been some impetus for a far-reaching set of reforms designed to tackle the issues mentioned.

> *e* The second paragraph shows good contextual awareness and a clear understanding of perspective. It attempts to highlight the political background to the Liberal social reforms without getting too bogged down in detail.

Despite 'new liberalism', the party and new government still had a traditional flavour, as epitomised by the prime minister Henry Campbell-Bannerman. This helps explain why some of the reforms appear to have been a compromise between comprehensive and limited provision. It should also be pointed out that individual measures were shaped by unique as well as more general influences in a number of cases, which can be traced back to the nineteenth century.

🖉 A sound analytical point emerges in this paragraph concerning the nature of 'new liberalism'. 'Unique and general influences' sounds a little vague, but this is likely to be developed later.

All of the social reforms displayed limitations. The education acts of 1906 and 1907, which introduced school meals and medical inspection, were both permissive in nature. Although the intention was to improve the health and welfare of a future generation, there was much opposition, especially with school meals, based on resentment at the suggestion that parents were failing to look after their children properly. The 1908 Old Age Pension Act applied only to those over 70 below a certain level of income, who could prove that they had been hard-working and law-abiding throughout their lives. National Insurance, introduced in 1911, only covered certain 'key' members of society: with health insurance it was the 'breadwinner' earning less than £160 per annum and with unemployment it was those working in occupations deemed to be most prone to fluctuations in the trade cycle. There was also much debate at the time over the fact that the scheme was contributory, with concern that the very poorest would not be able to pay.

🖉 This is an excellent paragraph, which develops the analytical approach started in the preceding paragraph. Notice how there is a focus on limitations and reference to particular reforms to support the argument. With this topic there can be a tendency to drift towards description of the reforms with a stab of evaluation at the end of each descriptive paragraph. This candidate is clearly avoiding falling into such a trap.

There were influencing factors, which gave something of an appearance that the reforms were a package. School meal provision was influenced by a Labour MP, and socialists in general had campaigned for non-contributory pension and insurance schemes. A general worry over health and fitness was again reflected in the child welfare measures, in turn influenced by the poor state of potential recruits to the Boer War (1899–1902), and health insurance. This was also tied up with concerns about maintaining an empire and Britain's standing as a major world economic and political power. It gives the impression that to some extent there was a coordinated attempt to lay a platform for something resembling what we would call a welfare state.

🖉 The candidate attempts to show how the reforms can be viewed as a planned programme and focuses on explanation. Maybe there could have been more detail on who influenced particular reforms and who exactly was expressing concern over Britain's world standing.

question

Each reform can also be seen as unique, however, with its own set of origins. The campaign for old age pensions was long and drawn out, and the final scheme was determined partly by ideas expounded by late nineteenth-century social reformers, such as Canon Barnett, but also by foreign example. Health insurance was also a reflection of foreign example and its implementation was affected by the need to acknowledge the power of friendly societies and industrial insurance companies. Thus, each reform could be viewed as a particular measure to deal with a particular problem under particular circumstances.

e This paragraph offers balanced comment, in contrast to the previous one. It considers the uniqueness of individual reforms, although the candidate might have expanded on the reference to foreign example by discussing, say, the influence of German social policy.

Despite the limitations and uniqueness of each reform, there were obvious signs that the reforms indicated a departure from *laissez-faire* individualism to a more state interventionist approach. With the school meals legislation the Liberals seemed to be arguing that the state knew best and was prepared to tackle the opposition from many parents, who believed they were being criticised for not caring for their children properly.

The Liberals were willing to make a substantial financial commitment to both old age pensions and National Insurance. Pensions were totally funded by the government and National Insurance through combinations of employer, employee and government contributions. All the social reforms indicated a willingness to improve the lot of more needy citizens, away from the stigma attached to the Poor Law.

In addition, where major criticisms occurred after the reforms there was a willingness to make amendments. This was true, for example, of pensions, whereby a clause — that anyone who had received Poor Law relief after 1 January 1908 would be excluded — was removed in 1911.

Finally, the Liberals were not afraid to find money for their reforms by using dramatic measures. The People's Budget of 1909 took money from the rich and gave to the poor by way of a series of land and property taxes. This upset wealthy members of society and the House of Lords vetoed the bill. The result was a major constitutional crisis, leading to the powers of the Lords being severely restricted. Although this can be seen as a personal attack by Lloyd George on the rich, it does indicate the extent to which the Liberals were willing to go to improve the positions of the poorest members of society.

e This is a very full and thrusting section, which argues how the reforms constituted a more collectivist approach to dealing with social issues. The argument is not explicitly linked with the term 'modern welfare state', but certainly builds on the material previously presented. It is hinting at the fact that the Liberals were attempting to make something of an optimum form of provision and were moving away from the permissive nature of nineteenth-century social legislation.

In conclusion, the Liberal social reforms had some resemblance to what we would know as a modern welfare state, but were unique to the early decades of the twentieth century. They were a response to issues that arose at that time. Due to conflicting ideology and restricted resources, the reforms constituted a compromise and a minimum form of provision. They laid something of a foundation for the post-Second World War welfare state, but certainly lacked the universal and comprehensive nature of the reforms that were introduced at that time.

e This conclusion brings together effectively the key parts of analysis from the main body of the answer. It gives a balanced judgement about what the Liberals did by suggesting that part of a foundation for a 'modern welfare state' was laid, but that this was a concept that was more acceptable to politicians and the general public at a later date. This is an impressive answer that focuses on explanation rather than description or narrative. There is a clear sense of judgement about what the Liberals intended to do. Historical detail is a bit thin, but overall this is a very proficient response. It is a 'best fit', not 'perfect fit', answer that falls into band I and there is no major reason why it would not have been awarded full marks, i.e. 45 (2 × 45 = 90). Better answers could be produced, but this does not detract from the fact that this is an excellent example of work produced by an AS candidate under exam constraints.

■ ■ ■

Band-III answer to question 1

The Liberals introduced many reforms from 1906 to 1914. They were due to pressure from the Labour Party and a concern that poverty was getting worse. There were also problems with Britain's position in the world. The reforms did lay a foundation for a modern welfare state, but there were some that had weaknesses.

e This introduction offers some balanced comment, but is rather vague and generalised. It is not exactly clear how the candidate intends to proceed.

The Liberals won a major election victory in 1906 and immediately started to introduce social reforms. They were worried that if they didn't, the Labour Party would promise to if they got into power. Labour had done well at the election and more working people had the vote so the Liberals had to appease them. In addition, there was competition from abroad, a problem in winning the Boer War, poverty surveys and rising infant mortality, all of which indicated that more had to be done for the poorest members of society.

e This section looks at the origins of the reforms in general terms, which could be of some relevance, but the material is not linked to the question.

The first reform was the School Meals Act of 1906, which allowed local authorities to provide free school meals for needy children. This was followed in 1907 with the introduction of medical inspection for schoolchildren.

In 1908 the Children Act was passed, which established juvenile courts and remand homes. It generally made parents more responsible for the behaviour of their children. All of these reforms for children laid the foundations of a welfare state to an extent, as they were not part of the Poor Law. But there were weaknesses. For example, not many authorities introduced school meals.

e This paragraph is quite detailed, but it is purely descriptive. Again, it needs to be linked with a line of argument.

Old age pensions came next in 1908. A pension of between 1s and 5s per week was introduced to those over 70 with incomes of less than £31 10s per year. They received it if they hadn't been drunk, or were aliens or were lazy. So the pension benefited the poor, but again had weaknesses, as it didn't cover all of the elderly.

e This follows in the same vein. The candidate gives more detailed and accurate description, but is falling into the trap of producing a narrative about the Liberal reforms.

In 1911 the Liberals introduced National Health Insurance. Workers aged 16 to 65 earning less than £160 per year had to pay 4d into a scheme. Employers paid 3d and the government 2d. Workers would then get benefits with 10s a week for men and 7s 6d for women, for 13 weeks. The benefits would change after that time. There was also a maternity grant for women and free medical treatment. This was important in an attempt to create a welfare state as it aimed to improve the health of many less well-off people away from the Poor Law. But it had weaknesses, such as the fact that the dependents of workers were not covered. In 1911 unemployment insurance was introduced for workers in selected jobs. Workers would again pay into a scheme and get benefits if they became unemployed. It covered jobs in industries where unemployment was most likely to occur. It was linked with the introduction of labour exchanges in 1909, which helped workers find jobs. There were also other minimum wages in sweated industries. All of these measures helped create a welfare state as they were designed to help a wider range of people to avoid the Poor Law.

e This is a highly detailed section on National Insurance and work-related reforms with some attempt to provide balanced analysis, i.e. there is a consideration of the weaknesses of the National Insurance Act. There is also some focus on the notion of a welfare state but, overall, emphasis is on describing what happened.

Another major social reform was the budget of 1909. This helped pay for the social reforms. It increased income tax, introduced a super-tax, raised death duties and made taxes on the land. It was introduced by the chancellor of the exchequer, Lloyd George, who wanted to take money away from the wealthy to give back to the poor. It caused problems and the Lords lost political powers after they refused to pass the legislation, which helped workers, such as the Trade Boards Act 1909, which fixed the budget. It was important as it showed the extent to which the government was willing to upset the rich to get its own way.

e The candidate gives an accurate account of the People's Budget, but it is not linked closely enough to the question. The material is relevant, but is simply included as part of the 'story'.

There were other reforms, such as those to do with housing and town planning, which also aimed to help working people. There was the beginning of the first 'garden city'. There was also a housing act in 1909, which gave authorities the power to pull down unsanitary houses. Again, these reforms were all part of an attempt to lay a foundation for a welfare state.

e Description of other reforms is tagged on here and contributes little to the overall answer. There is, however, an awareness that the reforms discussed may have contributed to a kind of welfare state.

In conclusion, the Liberals were pushed into laying a foundation for a welfare state by outside influences, such as the Labour Party. They needed to move people away from the Poor Law too because of the stigma attached to it. This meant that the population received more and better treatment and there was therefore a welfare state like we have today. But there were problems as not all local authorities had to provide school meals and not everyone was covered by insurance and pensions. So, to a great extent a modern welfare state wasn't created.

e In many ways the conclusion is effective and offers some balanced analytical explanation. It is rather vague, but there is indication that the candidate has understood the relevance of the material that has been described beforehand.

This answer is reasonably successful in evaluating key issues in so far as the relevant material is put together in a fairly tidy fashion, so that a logical and balanced conclusion can be achieved. It is a typical band-III answer in that it drifts towards description and narrative and the organisation is a bit uneven. There is a stab at analysis but no clear argument, and a limited attempt, mainly in the conclusion, to make a judgement about the relative importance of factors. Thus, this response would be awarded 28 marks (2 × 28 = 56).

Interwar domestic problems, 1918–39

Explain the causes of the 1926 General Strike.

■ ■ ■

Band-I answer to question 2

The term General Strike is misleading, as not all workers went on strike in 1926. The dispute was characterised by a call for support by the TUC from selected workers to support the miners, who had been 'locked out' by their employers. The strike was the result of a number of long-term, short-term and trigger factors. These related to the nature of the mining industry and the actions taken by employers, employees and governments over a period of time.

e This is a cogent, well-balanced introduction that explains the term 'General Strike', shows good awareness of the nature of causation and outlines key points to be discussed in the main body of the answer. It is just the right length, with no superfluous background material.

The General Strike lasted from 4 May to 13 May 1926. It was triggered by the actions of the Trades Union Congress in calling on workers from strategic industries to support the miners in their dispute with their employers. This, in turn, was deep-rooted, but it came to a head in April and May 1926, when both the miners and the mine owners reacted coolly to the recommendations of the Samuel Report. This had been set up to recommend how disputes between the two parties could be resolved, and suggested that in return for a national agreement on how the industry should operate, including a common approach to hours of work, the miners should accept a reduction in wages. The government wage subsidy would also end. This immediately prompted A. J. Cook, a prominent miners' leader, to say that his members would accept 'not a penny off the pay, not a minute on the day'. In reply, on 1 May 1926 the employers 'locked out' the miners.

e The answer proceeds by looking at the beginning of the strike with the intention of working backwards to chart its causes. This is a good strategy to use as it helps avoid a plodding narrative, parts of which are likely to be irrelevant. Maybe more could have been said about Cook and the miners' leadership, but this could be seen as nit-picking.

The strike was partly related to the nature of the mining industry and its historical development. From the miners' perspective coal mining had always been dangerous and very physically demanding work. They realised its importance for fuelling other industries, which dated back to the time of the industrial revolution, and emphasised the political and military significance of coal, which was illustrated during the First World War. Miners generally believed that they were never fairly treated and their demands for higher wages and shorter hours were made forcefully. By the 1920s the union of mine-workers, the Miners' Federation, had become quite a powerful organisation. It had secured improved conditions in 1919 with the passing of the Coal Mines Act, which established a 7-hour day and paved the way for state ownership. The union also forged strong links with other workers, most notably those employed in the transport industry, forming the Triple Alliance. But a major setback occurred on Black Friday (15 April 1921), when the miners were forced to accept wage cuts after the alliance broke down. This illustrated the strong position of employers, although the success of the Miners' Union was more generally governed by the state of the economy at any one point in time.

e There is some drift towards narrative in this paragraph in an attempt to discuss the long-term causes of the strike. There is also a fair amount of generalisation that could have been clarified with a little more historical detail.

The mining industry had always been in private ownership, with a temporary and partial take-over by the state during and shortly after the First World War. The owners ran an industry that was fraught with technological difficulties. Deeper mines created greater problems as regards extraction, and as time went by the finite nature of coal was increasingly recognised. Although output continued to grow during the early twentieth century, there were significant fluctuations in profit levels due to foreign competition. It has been argued, however, that owners could have invested more in the industry to keep up with rivals but failed to do so. At times there seemed to be a preference to reduce costs, which included expanding the working day and paying miners less. This was certainly the case in 1921, and again in 1925. Like the miners and their leaders, there was a certain unwillingness to compromise and conflict seemed inevitable.

e This is a good paragraph that discusses the position of the employers and links this with the question in the final sentence. Again, there is some generalisation, but this is acceptable when discussing a long-term causal factor such as this.

Another longer-term factor related to the role of governments. The first Labour government, formed in 1924, was sympathetic towards the miners, but it was short-lived. Conservative governments of the early and mid-1920s took a harder line, as illustrated by Baldwin's support for the employers during the summer of 1925. The Conservative government of 1925 also decided to return to the Gold Standard, which made British exports more expensive and therefore had a detrimental effect on the coal industry. Baldwin's government also had an important role to play in the months leading up to the strike.

e The discussion here turns to the role of governments in dealing with the problem of mining. Although a bit thin on the Labour Party stance, it links material on the return to the Gold Standard with the position of the coal industry, which is impressive.

The effects of returning to the Gold Standard really took a hold by the summer of 1925. The profits of mining started to fall, mine owners pushed for cuts in wages and longer hours, and threatened workers with the prospect of unemployment. The miners, the TUC and other unions were opposed. Despite the initial support for the employers from Baldwin, the Conservative government decided on 31 July, Red Friday, to subsidise miners' wages for 9 months while an investigation was carried out. It was chaired by Sir Herbert Samuel, a Liberal, with a brief to identify the problems of the industry and report on how they could be resolved. In March he reported and made some concessions to both the owners and the miners, which were outlined earlier. Probably his most important recommendation was that there needed to be considerable reorganisation of the industry, but under private ownership. The recommendations proved to be unacceptable to both parties. It is, however, often claimed that the real significance of the commission was that it gave the government time to prepare for a general strike, which had originally been hinted at. An Organisation for the Maintenance of Supplies (OMS) was formed and the country was divided into ten regional 'action' areas, each of which would be governed by a civil commissioner and policed by special constables and the armed forces. This provides some credence for the view that the government had limited faith in the Samuel Commission and wanted to inflict some kind of defeat on the miners. In fact, the TUC indicated that it was willing to negotiate a truce right up to the eve of the strike, but Baldwin refused to negotiate, particularly after printers at the *Daily Mail* refused to produce a paper that condemned the strike. Thus, on 4 May 1926 the General Strike went ahead.

This is a lengthy section that builds nicely on what has gone before. There is some description but the focus is on explaining the deteriorating relationship between the government, the TUC, employers and employees. Although this is not clearly signposted, the candidate is obviously looking at short-term factors. The trigger for the strike was discussed in the second paragraph and is not repeated here, which is a good indication of effective planning.

It would be easy to blame Baldwin and his government for provoking the strike so that there would be an excuse for attempting to suppress the political power of the unions. Both the miners' leaders and employers displayed intransigence, however, and are partly to blame for the conflict. The TUC emerged with some credibility, as it attempted to negotiate a peaceful settlement. Only the miners themselves can be found to be blameless, as they appeared to be victims of political bickering and economic circumstance.

The conclusion is balanced, but could be criticised for offering no major judgement about the causes of the strike. How factors are linked has been addressed to an extent, but not explicitly enough to warrant a very high band-I mark. This answer would therefore achieve 40 marks (2 × 40 = 80).

■ ■ ■

Band-III answer to question 2

The 1926 General Strike happened for a number of reasons. It was due partly to the actions of the mine owners, but also to the miners. The government had a role to play too.

e A fairly bland introduction 'signposts' and almost states the obvious. It is not clear that the concept of causation is understood, although there is an appreciation that a number of factors need to be considered.

After the First World War the miners were in a strong position as they had contributed to the war effort and their services were still in demand. During the war the mining industry had been nationalised, but this was changed in 1921 when it was put back into private hands. In 1919 the Sankey Commission recommended improvements, including a 7-hour day, and some of these were included in the Coal Mines Act of 1919. But in 1920 a trade depression happened and the demand for coal fell. The mine owners wanted to reduce wages but the miners' union opposed this. There was support for the miners from other unions, such as the National Union of Railway Workers and transport workers, which resulted in the Triple Alliance. In the end, the miners accepted lower wages. This created a grievance among miners and was a reason for the General Strike in 1926.

e This is a detailed section that is accurate, relevant and generally well written. Unfortunately, it is also a classic example of telling a story about the topic in the question in the hope that it results in an answer. There is little indication of an understanding of longer-term causal factors either. The focus on the question at the end of the paragraph seems to be tagged on. 'Created a grievance' is rather vague and could have been explained more fully to make the whole paragraph more pertinent.

In 1925 Britain returned to the Gold Standard, which made coal more expensive for foreigners. Mine owners again tried to reduce wages. This was supported by Stanley Baldwin, the prime minister, and his Conservative government. He talked about the need to make sacrifices at a difficult time. The miners were once again angry and there was talk of a general strike. The government announced there would be an investigation into mining conditions and set up the Samuel Commission. In March 1926 the commission reported and said the miners should accept lower wages and that government subsidies to the mining industry would stop. It also said there shouldn't be long hours for miners and that there should be more national agreement over conditions. The miners and the mine owners didn't like the recommendations and this caused more disagreement. There was a deadlock and this was another reason for the General Strike.

e The candidate produces more of the same here, i.e. much description and narrative, although it is accurate and the material continues to be relevant. The results of the Samuel Commission are explained carefully, but the response of the employers and employees is described in a rather vague fashion.

The government had tried to delay the strike, but it was almost inevitable. The Trades Union Congress (TUC) also tried to negotiate a deal between the miners and mine owners but failed. Baldwin did not seem to want to agree with the TUC and made plans for the nation to cope with a strike. The country was divided into ten areas that would be organised by special police.

question

The story continues. This section is rather thin on details of the government's contingency plans and contains no clear explanation of why Baldwin attempted to delay the implementation of the Samuel Commission's recommendations.

The final straw for the miners was when mine owners shut them out from the pits. The TUC then organised a strike, but tried to negotiate with Baldwin. The prime minister was no longer interested in talking. He was upset over events at the *Daily Mail*, where workers refused to print a story about the miners that was critical. In fact, by this time he was obsessed with a Communist threat and saw the miners' dispute as the possible start of a revolution. Communists had already been arrested in 1925.

This section contains an interesting comment on the 'red scare' factor, although it is generalised and largely unsubstantiated. This point could have been expanded on to strengthen the answer, but the paragraph ends bluntly.

The strike got underway on 4 May 1926, although not all workers went on strike. The government was very well organised and used the Army to get supplies through. They also made good use of the media, particularly with their own newspaper, the *British Gazette*. The BBC also seemed to be biased towards the government. On 12 May 1926 the TUC called the strike off, as it didn't seem to be working. But the miners carried on until November, and when they returned they had to accept lower wages and increased hours. This showed how tough the owners were and supports the view that they were partly responsible for the strike.

This paragraph illustrates a common fault with answers to questions that demand discussion of causation. The candidate has moved on to describe events during the strike, which are not relevant. There is an attempt to link this with the question, but this is done rather loosely. Little is added to the quality of the answer by doing this.

The mine owners caused the strike because they were unwilling to listen to the miners and took harsh action against them. The miners were also responsible, as they seemed unreasonable and not willing to compromise. The government also caused the strike, as Baldwin could not work out a deal with the TUC. The government was also very well organised, which meant the strike was doomed to fail.

The conclusion at last highlights the role of the government, miners and mine owners in the strike, but makes no reasoned judgement about who or what was most responsible. It is rather vague and woolly too. It does, however, at least recognise the need to deal with a number of factors.

This answer illustrates an important point relating to narrative. The material used here is relevant and directed towards the question through a chronological story. There is a stab at analysis, although this is not clearly evident. But it also contains an example of irrelevant narrative and description in the penultimate paragraph; even though the historical detail may be accurate, this section would be unlikely to get much above band V. The answer would have been given 27 marks (2 × 27 = 54), and therefore a low band III overall.

Foreign policy, 1939–63

Assess the reasons why Britain's attitude to European cooperation changed in the period 1945–63.

■ ■ ■

Band-1 answer to question 3

After the end of the Second World War there was a general view in Britain that there should be a degree of cooperation in Europe, partly to help nations get back on their feet but also to prevent the prospect of another war. By the early 1950s there was a lack of clarity over how Britain would play a role in cooperation and a reluctance to join organisations formed by other European countries. This was due mainly to a fear of losing control over British affairs, particularly those of an economic nature. By 1961 attitudes had changed again as British politicians displayed a wish to be an integral part of the European Economic Community. This resulted from a realisation of the economic benefits of cooperation and a wish not to fall behind European neighbours.

e The answer starts positively by setting the scene and identifying the change in attitude. The importance of economic factors is emphasised, but there is scant mention of other issues such as Britain's relationship with the USA and the strategic significance of empire.

By 1946 there was talk in Britain of the need to cooperate within Europe to form a 'United States of Europe', and in 1947 Winston Churchill chaired a United European Committee, which aimed to put this idea into operation. Clement Attlee, the Labour prime minister, was rather cool on the idea but by 1948 had developed his own idea of a 'Western union', which would unify Europe over a range of economic, political, social and military affairs. At this stage, a major obstacle to cooperation was that there was no clear idea of what it involved. In Britain it was viewed as necessary as long as the British did not lose their identity.

e This is a clearly written paragraph, which explains Britain's position at the end of the Second World War. It touches on the issue of 'national sovereignty', which determined the British reaction to plans for cooperation up to 1963. No real problems here.

Nevertheless, Britain made further attempts to cooperate over military and economic affairs. This is shown by Britain's involvement in the formation of the North Atlantic Treaty Organisation (NATO), discussions over a European Defence Community and participation in the Organisation for European Economic Cooperation (OEEC). Despite this, it could be argued that Britain's involvement was driven by a need to cooperate more with America than Europe, as NATO provided American military support to Europe and the OEEC was set up to administer American economic aid under the Marshall Plan. This was linked with the so-called 'special relationship' with America, and was a main factor in determining the level of cooperation to which Britain was committed up to 1963.

e Britain's 'special relationship with America' is highlighted as a key point. The candidate clearly understands the concept of continuity and uses a range of historical facts to support the argument. More could have been said about how the 'special relationship' came about, with more focused analysis of its importance.

Another influencing factor that emerged early on was the difference in attitude between political parties in Britain. By the early 1950s the Conservatives appeared more pro-Europe than Labour. In 1948 Attlee had refused to attend a congress in The Hague, led by Churchill, which proposed the setting up of a kind of European parliament. Eventually, a Council of Europe was created, which consisted of representatives from parliaments of member nations, including Britain. Attlee did not treat it seriously, as it was simply a forum for debate and lacked decision-making powers. Although there were differences in attitude between Conservatives and Labour, this was probably not a major factor in influencing cooperation. The differences were rather false and due more to party political infighting than fundamental disagreement over European cooperation.

e This very effective paragraph shows how there were differences of opinion between political parties in Britain over the issue of European cooperation. There is judgement about the importance of this factor, although there is no attempt to link it with other factors.

Immediately after the war, the need to maintain something of an empire was considered important by British politicians, as it provided an established market for finished goods and a source of raw materials. Far more people lived in the empire than Europe and it was therefore seen as still having much more economic potential. But the grip on empire started to loosen as member nations looked to gain independence and the financial cost of policing it grew. By the early 1960s most of it had been dismantled, leaving a Commonwealth, or loose collection of ex-empire nations, that showed a willingness to cooperate over economic affairs. This eased Britain's commitments and made politicians realise the significance of the growing European Economic Community.

e The focus here is on the role of empire; the point is developed carefully and is explained fully. More could have been made of the notion of a 'wind of change' and how this affected the Conservatives' views about cooperation after 1957. This could have been linked to the early comments on party differences.

The relative success of the European Coal and Steel Community (ECSC), formed in 1951, was also important in forcing Britain to take more of a positive view towards Europe. Ironically, Britain was excluded from the initial negotiations over a plan that would enable freer trade of coal and steel between selected European nations (France and Germany to begin with) and signify the beginnings of a more united Europe. Britain was asked to join at a later date but refused, as it was thought that there would be a loss of national sovereignty and that the newly nationalised coal industry in Britain would suffer. By the mid-1950s members of the ECSC had been so impressed by the benefits of belonging that they looked to widen its scope. This caused something of a rethink among British politicians, although the issue of national sovereignty was still the main barrier to renegotiating acceptance.

e The discussion here revolves around the significance of the ECSC. The candidate links this to the question of national sovereignty and suggests that the development of the ECSC was a turning-point. So, although a chronological approach is being adopted, the answer remains relevant.

A major turning-point occurred in March 1957 when the Treaty of Rome was signed, which established the European Economic Community (EEC). The aim was to create a 'free' market for member nations, which would allow for the easier flow of a greater and cheaper range of goods. A supranational administrative and governing structure was outlined, which would be used to run the EEC. Again, Britain declined to take part, as it feared that the 'supranational' bodies would take power away from British political institutions, Britain's empire would be damaged and British farmers would be worse off than foreign counterparts. Britain had, once again, 'missed the bus'.

e This describes the origins and nature of the EEC, but again links the material successfully with the question. The point about damage to British farming could have been explained, as this was always a contentious issue.

Within 2 years, though, Macmillan's Conservative government had taken a U-turn and decided to apply to join the EEC. Attitudes had changed quite suddenly as there was a fear that Britain would be excluded from trading with the EEC. There was also concern over the fact that the British-backed counter-version, entitled EFTA (European Free Trade Area), was considered far less effective and significant. Macmillan's U-turn was strengthened by the fact that his cabinet, Parliament, his party and the general public all gave a fair degree of backing to the plan. The declining significance of empire added extra weight to the case. Unfortunately for Macmillan, an application to join was rejected, mainly due to the objections of founder members France and Germany. This was formally announced in January 1963.

e The full and coherent explanation of Macmillan's U-turn in this paragraph leads on nicely from the analysis of the EEC. More detailed evidence could have been provided to back up arguments about fear over lost trade and the declining importance of empire. Nevertheless, this is a very sound, analytical paragraph.

Macmillan was devastated by the decision. He and other politicians had been worried about the tenuous 'special relationship' with America and had witnessed how the EEC had seemingly strengthened the positions of France and Germany in Europe. Western Europe had quickly become a lucrative market with considerable purchasing power, exceeding that of the Commonwealth. All of this convinced Macmillan that a change in attitude was correct but he had been defeated, partly due to a reaction against the more entrenched and stubborn views held by politicians from an earlier era.

e This shows good insight and awareness of change and continuity. Links are made between a number of factors previously discussed.

Thus, probably the most important reason why Britain's attitude changed was that western Europe became a more lucrative economic market than the British empire. There was also a fear that Britain would lose out politically to France and Germany. The question of loss of national sovereignty never disappeared, which suggests there wasn't a total change in attitude and which might help explain why the application to join was rejected in 1963. There were, however, other more deep-rooted political reasons for this.

e This is a solid conclusion, which makes a clear judgement about the merits of the reasons discussed.

Overall, this is obviously a band-I answer that covers much ground, makes links between key issues and finishes with a precise and well-stated judgement. The only real criticism is that some of the arguments expounded could have been supported with a bit more evidence. The candidate would not therefore quite gain full marks: this answer would be awarded 42 marks (2 × 42 = 84 overall).

■ ■ ■

Band-III answer to question 3

At the end of the Second World War Britain was in a strong position, having won the war. It had worked closely with the Allies to defeat Germany but there were now more pressing problems, such as the home economy and social policy, that had to be focused on. This meant there was no need to cooperate closely with Europe. But by 1963 the European Economic Community had been formed and Britain then wanted to join. There were many reasons why Britain changed its mind to work with other European countries more closely.

e The answer starts quite well, with focused and balanced comment. A weakness is that the reasons for a change in attitude are not outlined and therefore it is not clear what line of argument the candidate is going to adopt. It 'signposts', i.e. points the reader towards the obvious.

At the end of the war Winston Churchill wanted to make sure another major conflict didn't occur and was keen on the idea of western European countries working together to defend each other if one single nation was attacked. Britain also supported NATO, which involved America supporting western Europe in times of conflict. Not all politicians agreed on this approach. Clement Attlee, the prime minister from 1945 to 1951, was unsure about the 'special relationship' that Churchill believed existed between America and Britain. Attlee was not as trustful of America as Churchill and thought that they were always looking to take advantage of situations in Europe. This helps us understand why Britain was not keen to cooperate with Europe.

✏ The candidate makes a clear statement of Britain's position at the end of the war, concentrating on defence and relationships with America. The answer tends slightly towards description but then offers more analytical explanation in the last sentence.

In 1951 the European Coal and Steel Community was formed. It started with France and Germany. France thought that by cooperating with Germany there would be less likelihood of Germany dominating the rest of Europe again. This plan by Robert Schuman was hatched without consulting Britain, although it was discussed with America. In fact, the French and Germans didn't really want Britain to join. Attlee refused to join anyway. He argued that it would lead to Britain losing power and the British coal industry would be badly affected. This was a good example of how Britain didn't cooperate with Europe.

✏ A full but rather weak section as it describes rather than explains Britain's attitude towards Europe in the early 1950s. More could have been made of the French and German views on the British position.

Attlee also dismissed the idea of cooperation over the Pleven Plan. This was an idea about producing a common European army and again had the support of America. Attlee thought it wasn't practical and couldn't see how it would work.

✏ This may be relevant but the candidate hasn't stated why.

By the end of 1951 Britain was said to have missed the European bus for the first time. It 'missed the bus' again in 1957 when it decided not to join the EEC (European Economic Community). This was an extension of the ECSC and aimed to provide a 'common market' for all the member countries. This meant that goods could be sold and bought more cheaply, which would help the economies of the countries that joined. Standards of living would rise. It was thought that if western Europe was stronger economically, there would be less chance of another war. Britain again did not want to join with the countries as it thought there would be a loss of national power and prestige. So Britain formed its own version of the EEC called EFTA (European Free Trade Association) in January 1960. It consisted of Britain, Norway, Denmark, Sweden, Austria, Portugal and Switzerland. These were all countries that had refused to join the EEC. They too were worried about the European Commission and courts and how this would have affected their own parliaments. EFTA was important as it shows that Britain was willing to cooperate with Europe at this time, but not with the EEC as it was afraid of losing power.

✏ This section contains much factual material but it is not directed towards the question. There is mention of the potential loss of national power and prestige half-way through and this is repeated at the end, but this point is not developed. The candidate obviously knows about the topic but has failed to use the material effectively.

Within a few years, however, Britain had made a U-turn and changed its mind about the EEC. The government decided it wanted to join as it would provide more economic opportunities and, besides, EFTA wasn't working very well. Britain's empire was weakening too, and it no longer provided a secure market.

question

 The answer is beginning to fade away and although some relevant points are made, they lack substance. This is a disappointingly thin paragraph that keeps the response in the middle band.

Although Britain wanted to join, the French leader, de Gaulle, opposed the application. France had been wary of Britain's relationship with America, especially over nuclear weapons. De Gaulle thought the British should have worked more closely with France and until they showed they wanted to he would persist by opposing their entry to the EEC.

 This statement about de Gaulle's reaction to Britain's application for membership adds little weight to the answer. The point about the need to work more closely with France is interesting, but is not expanded.

Britain's attitude to cooperating with Europe changed a lot from 1945 to 1963. This was due to a number of factors such as winning the war, the relationship with America and the change in importance of empire. Individual politicians were also significant. Probably the most important reason was that Britain started to feel weak, but there is no agreement over this question.

 A range of reasons is outlined in the conclusion, with some attempt at judgement. However, it is quite a limp ending that has no thrust to it.

The essay is reasonably successful in so far as there is some attempt at evaluating key issues. The level of understanding again is reasonable, but the big weakness is that it veers towards describing what happened rather than explaining why. It recognises the need to deal with a range of factors and there is a limited attempt to highlight the most important ones. Therefore, this script would have been awarded a band-III mark of 29 (2 × 29 = 58).

Postwar Britain, 1945–64

Assess the reasons for the Labour election victory of 1945.

■ ■ ■

Band-I answer to question 4

The Labour Party won a remarkable landslide election victory in 1945, mainly as a result of promising a far-reaching programme of social reform. The Second World War had caused much destruction and disruption and the British population wanted to look forward to a new and prosperous future. This needs to be considered alongside the opinion of Churchill and the Conservatives, who took a more cautious view of reform and were more moderate in their proposals for how the nation was to be reconstructed.

e This is an excellent beginning that displays clear focus and a good awareness of perspective and balance. It is evident that the candidate is likely to be in control of the argument from the beginning.

In the run up to the general election of July 1945 the Labour Party produced its plan for social reform in the election manifesto entitled 'Let Us Face the Future'. This was based partly on the proposals made by William Beveridge in his 1942 report, where he stated the need to tackle the five giants in society (want, squalor, idleness, ignorance, disease) using a universal and comprehensive approach to social policy. The report had been greeted with widespread support from the British people and Labour knew this. Labour politicians also realised that the Conservatives, particularly Churchill, had been rather negative about Beveridge's proposals. Churchill likened the plan to Utopia and El Dorado, i.e. 'pie in the sky' views of what could and should be achieved in the future. Thus, Labour saw that they could exploit the report for political as well as ideological reasons.

e In this paragraph the candidate discusses Labour's adoption of the Beveridge Report and how this was a likely vote-winner. There could have been some indication of the degree of support for Beveridge by making reference to the public response through the media and opinion polls. The explanation of Churchill's response is a bit weak too. More could have been made at this point about his role as Conservative Party leader and wartime prime minister.

Labour's manifesto gave an indication of how a 'welfare state' would be introduced. There was to be a National Health Service providing free health care, a comprehensive National Insurance scheme and National Assistance to act as a safety net for those not covered by other measures. Underpinning this was an economic policy that promised a move towards full employment. Labour also showed a willingness to provide more housing and to build on the provisions of the 1944 Education Act, which

question

made secondary education free for all. These promises seemed far-reaching and were aimed at creating a society that would experience living standards not dreamt of before the war.

> *e* This expands on the issue of Labour's promise to the electorate. Although Labour's plan for a 'welfare state' is described, there is a solid piece of analysis at the end.

There were many people who still saw state intervention as taboo, as it was an infringement of individual rights and possibly encouraged idleness and a lack of self-reliance. To an extent, Labour was able to overcome such fears by exploiting the shared adversity experienced during the war years. All classes in society were affected to a greater or lesser extent by the Blitz, evacuation, rationing, conscription and a general feeling of austerity. This made it easier for the people to understand each other's plight and the concept of universality became more acceptable. A good example of this was evacuation, which acted as an eye-opener to the rural middle classes who took in many working-class children from deprived urban areas. As some historians have pointed out, however, this shouldn't be exaggerated as evacuation was relatively short-lived and the experiences of evacuees were mixed. Thus, Labour's collectivist (i.e. intervention on behalf of the whole of society) policy became more acceptable and for many was essential if Britain was to remain a great nation. The notion of fair and equal treatment was not linked so much with extreme left-wing views, and was seen simply as the appropriate stance to take at the time.

> *e* The candidate gives a strong explanation of why Labour's policies were likely to be accepted and gain votes. The issue of opposition to their plans could have been explored further, highlighting the role of particular individuals, such as Churchill. The links between the Blitz, rationing, conscription and shared adversity could also have been explored further, in the same manner as evacuation.

Labour's victory was also aided by the fact that there was no real socialist alternative. The Liberals, who had once been the party for working people, were a spent force and the other socialist groups that did exist were very small and insignificant.

> *e* A fair point, but 'other socialist groups' is rather vague and ought to have been explained further. Examples would have strengthened the point being made.

Worries over Labour's ability to govern were now far less than they had been. Labour had experience of government in the interwar years and had been reasonably successful, despite the split caused by MacDonald's 'betrayal' to head a Conservative-dominated National Government. Senior Labour politicians had also performed well during the war years, which gave the public confidence.

> *e* Another relevant point is made, which mentions both the prewar and wartime situations. The first sentence could have been clarified by spelling out the perceived 'red threat' before the war.

Conservative Party weaknesses had a role in ensuring a Labour victory. The party was still associated with the interwar depression years. It was the party that had been most dominant during that period but had failed to tackle economic problems effectively, especially unemployment. Although, ironically, living standards had improved, there were signs that society was divided and that some people, especially in the south, had benefited more than others. The Conservative Party and wartime leader Winston Churchill was a hero in so far as Britain was deemed to have won the war. But Churchill took a negative and rather pessimistic view of Labour's plans and used scaremongering tactics to discredit them. He suggested that Labour would lead the nation towards totalitarianism as seen in Germany under Hitler, whereby the state would have total control over the lives of people. There is some evidence to suggest that this tactic shocked and angered members of the electorate. It is likely, though, that most people did not take much notice. Churchill was probably being cautious, as he didn't want to make promises that could not be kept. For most of the war period his primary objective was simply to win the war. Therefore, we must not exaggerate the importance of his outburst in the run up to the election.

e The focus in this section is on explaining Conservative weaknesses. It is clearly written, with sound judgement and balanced analysis. A criticism is that it lacks detail to back up some of the points made, particularly with respect to interwar economic performance and the wartime comments made by Churchill.

To conclude, Labour's landslide victory of 1945 was mainly due to the radical social reform programme that it promised at a time of high expectation. This was strengthened by the fact that the Conservative Party was cautious over reform and that there was no other viable option presented by any of the other parties.

e The conclusion is solid, without being over-sophisticated. A focused judgement is made and links the strengths of Labour with the weaknesses of the Conservatives. The connecting of issues does not occur throughout the whole answer, however — there are signs that the candidate realises the importance of this but does not achieve it. Therefore, this answer would be placed at the lower end of band I and receive 38 marks (2 × 38 = 76).

■ ■ ■

Band-III answer to question 4

Labour clearly won the election of 1945 due to a number of reasons. It promised a better future and seemed to have the more able politicians to make this happen. The Conservatives, on the other hand, were weak and not in touch with the public.

e The introduction attempts to outline how the question is likely to be tackled, but it is rather vague. The first sentence is obvious, and 'signposts'.

The Labour Party easily won the 1945 general election. It won 393 seats compared with the Conservatives, who won 213. Therefore it was a landslide victory. This triumph was a result of the war. During the Second World War, investigations showed that there was a need to improve policies to help everyone in society. William

Beveridge outlined a plan to attack five evils in society, which were connected with poverty. Labour adopted his plan as it fitted in with the party's own ideas. The party knew it would be popular with the public, especially during the war. Therefore, at the end of the war Labour promised to carry out social reforms that would improve living and working conditions for everyone. This appealed to many voters, especially the working class, and was an obvious reason why people voted for Labour.

e There is some explanation within this narrative/descriptive approach, but the answer so far lacks sustained, relevant analysis.

Labour promised to build more and better houses, to introduce an NHS and provide free schooling. It also promised to get rid of unemployment, which had been a major problem in the interwar years. This is another reason why it gained much support.

e This is a very short paragraph that outlines the welfare state. There is a 'bolt-on' sentence that attempts to link the material to the question, but no explanation.

The British people were happy to vote Labour, as the party now seemed less of a threat. Before, it was associated with communism and trade union activity, such as strikes. At the end of the war it seemed far more responsible. Some of its politicians, such as Ernest Bevin, had done well in the war. They showed that they were able and professional and would make Britain great again.

e A fair point is being made in this section, but there is a lack of evidence to support it. For example, more could have been said about the work of Bevin and examples given of 'able and professional' activity.

Another reason why Labour won so convincingly was that the Liberal Party, one of Labour's challengers, was a small party that had been declining before the war. Although the Liberals were sympathetic to Labour's ideas, they were not 'new' and dynamic like Labour and therefore did not appeal to the electorate as much. They also didn't enter as many candidates for election.

e This section includes relevant comment, but again there is a lack of strong explanation. For example, by not entering as many candidates for election it was likely that Liberal supporters would vote Labour rather than Conservative, as their values and policies had some similarity. This should have been spelt out.

The weaknesses of the Conservatives also help explain a Labour victory. Winston Churchill, the Conservative Party leader, was not keen on reform. He criticised the Beveridge Report and, in fact, didn't realise that Beveridge was going to make such a plan. Beveridge was only expected to investigate insurance but he ended up planning an attack on poverty. Churchill was unhappy about this as he thought it would take people's attention away from winning the war. Churchill also made adverse comments about the Labour Party and called them Nazis. This was not a good idea at a time when Britain had just defeated Hitler and Nazism. The Conservatives did not really have a radical plan of their own either, although Butler had introduced an important Education Act in 1944. This raised the school-leaving age, introduced the tripartite system and made education free for everyone in society. It was considered a major breakthrough and was welcomed by everyone.

e This is quite a full paragraph that develops the issue of Conservative weakness in a logical manner. It is detailed and accurate, but there is a tendency towards description. It would have been better if the material had been more directed at the question, and comparison made with Labour strengths.

The Labour Party won the general election in 1945 for a number of reasons. The most important was its social reform programme, which created a 'welfare state'. The weaknesses of the Conservatives also played a part, although they did have some success in the field of education. All in all, Labour's strengths were more important than Conservative weaknesses.

e This succinct conclusion covers a range of issues. A clear judgement is made but the answer ends rather bluntly. There is recognition of the need to deal with a number of factors, but there is very little explanation of the most important linkages. The strength of this answer is its cogency and clarity, which takes it to the higher end of band III. It would achieve 30 marks (2 × 30 = 60).